Less is More

The overwhelming power of God's simplicity

S. Sekou Abodunrin

Less Is More
Sekou Publishing
sekou@sekou.me

Copyright © 2013 by Sekou Abodunrin
All designs by Zen77 www.zen77world.com
ISBN: 978-0-9575677-0-2

Published by Sekou Publishing.
All rights reserved.

Unless otherwise indicated, all Scripture quotations are taken from the King James Version of the bible.

Some Scripture quotations marked (WUEST) are taken from The New Testament: An Expanded Translation (WET) by Kenneth S. Wuest. Copyright © 2000 2010 Wm. B. Eerdmans Publishing Company.

Some Scripture quotations marked (AMP) are taken from the Amplified® Bible, Copyright © 1954, 1958, 1962, 1964, 1965, 1987 by The Lockman Foundation. Used by permission.
www.lockman.org

The author has emphasised some words in Scripture quotations in bold type.

Introduction

The teaching on the parable of the unjust judge was delivered in various meetings in its spoken form. We have put this into book form, and you hold this in your hands to study and learn that there is no darkness in the heart of God.

There are some well-meaning people who suppose that God is sometimes good and at other times bad. That view is wholly compatible with our misconceptions and our attempts to make sense of God in the light of our experiences and sentiments. I have no sympathy for this view and think it untenable especially because we have seen Jesus who is the only one who has seen the Father. Jesus is not sometimes promoting evil and at other times doing good. What we have seen of Jesus' character has set the standard for what God must be like.

What is projected about God in the bible is a progressive revelation that finds its clearest expression in Christ Jesus. It is our belief that God cannot be anything different from Jesus of Nazareth. The issue that we face in this little book is how to use Jesus as the template for gaining a clearer understanding of what God is really like. It is our hope that the reader can track the flight of our intention to its appointed target: exploring the goodness of God in the face of seeming contradiction. God is infinitely satisfied in his own goodness, now it is your turn to maximize your joy by resting in the goodness of God.

Open your mouth and taste,

open your eyes and see—

how good God is.

Blessed are you who run to him.

Psalm 34:8 (The Message)

And it is this message which we
have heard from Him and at
present is ringing in our ears and
we are bringing back tidings to
you, that God as to His nature is
light, and darkness in Him does
not exist, not even one particle.

1 John 1:5 (Wuest)

Acknowledgements

To Olatundun,

You love and support me in countless ways through all my various disappearances into writing, musing, meditating and many things unprintable. Let it be said that I have found in you an excellent wife who is far more precious than jewels.

Emi and Adun,

You graciously share your dad. How can I ever repay? You are my crash course in relearning the fatherhood of God.

The Good God

1 And he spake a parable unto them to this end, that men ought always to pray, and not to faint;

2 Saying, There was in a city a judge, which feared not God, neither regarded man:

3 And there was a widow in that city; and she came unto him, saying, Avenge me of mine adversary.

4 And he would not for a while: but afterward he said within himself, Though I fear not God, nor regard man;

5 Yet because this widow troubleth me, I will avenge her, lest by her continual coming she weary me.

6 And the Lord said, Hear what the unjust judge saith.

7 And shall not God avenge his own elect, which cry day and night unto him, though he bear long with them?

8 I tell you that he will avenge them speedily. Nevertheless when the Son of man cometh, shall he find faith on the earth?

Luke 18: 1-7 (KJV)

The greatest decisions that you can make in life are to be a student of God's word, and to allow its ideas shape your thinking and govern your walk. The challenge with this particular parable of Jesus is that so much has been written about it, so that every time we read or hear about it, we are convinced all over again of the validity of what we have heard in previous sermons. This hinders us from actually reading the holy writ afresh. This is the challenge of familiarity. It is the greatest hindrance to receiving further light.

There is a three-pronged challenge here. The first has to do with the nature of parables. The church has not done too well with parables or anything having to do with symbolic language in general. This much is evident in the various treatments and interpretations of the book of Revelations and the prophetic scriptures. Symbolic things get muddled up and we sometimes end up with some weird stuff especially when it comes to application and practice.

The second challenge is that unlike other parables, this particular parable concerning the widow and the judge only appears in one book in the whole Bible. It might have been easier if John, Matthew or Mark also treated it. Their treatment of the parable might have given us a glimpse that allows us to easily unlock the true meaning. Since this parable is recorded in only one place, we have to start with what we know from the clear teaching of scripture in order to unravel this parable. We will use what we know to unravel the unknown.

The third challenge is typical of Luke the gospel writer.

> **While Matthew and Mark use direct representation to teach, Luke leans heavily on the use of contrasts to communicate the truths in his parables.**

This is Luke's signature style and we do well to remember this fact. It is therefore important that you understand that this parable is one of contrasts. If this pivotal point is missed, and we treat this as a direct illustration, we reach conclusions that do not do justice to the fuller revelation of God in his holy word. Luke's use of contrasts can be illustrated from another parable of Luke concerning prayer.

2 And he said unto them, When ye pray, say, Our Father which art in heaven, Hallowed be thy name. Thy kingdom come. Thy will be done, as in heaven, so in earth. 5 And he said unto them, Which of you shall have a friend, and shall go unto him at midnight, and say unto him, Friend, lend me three loaves;

6 For a friend of mine in his journey is come to me, and I have nothing to set before him?

7 And he from within shall answer and say, Trouble me not: the door is now shut, and my children are with me in bed; I cannot rise and give thee.

8 I say unto you, Though he will not rise and give him, because he is his friend, yet because of his importunity he will rise and give him as many as he needeth.

Luke 11:2, 5, 6-8 (KJV)

Jesus is shedding more light on his disciples concerning prayer. The things he teaches here are in addition to the concepts that he had taught them earlier from the Sermon on the Mount. The context is that Jesus is teaching the disciples how to pray, and he is specifically instructing them about approaching Jehovah as Father in prayer. He wants to drive home the point, so he uses a parable to illustrate it. Jesus weaves the point into a story that asks a question of his hearers. I suggest that you also place yourself in the shoes of a hearer, ponder upon and answer that question. The lesson learnt hinges on it.

He communicated this truth by asking a key question: "which of you shall have a friend?" This friend in bed has been approached at midnight and the request is just for three loaves! The request was not for his house or livelihood- it was just for three loaves of bread. He should have been more sympathetic of the one making the request but clearly he wasn't. Jesus has deliberately formulated the parable to stir a specific response in the hearer.

The intention was for the hearers to formulate an answer along the lines of "No, I will not have that kind of friend" or, "Yes, I have that kind of friend."

This friend is rude. He is not even much of a friend anyway. He does not get up to see his friend who was at the door. His reasons were down to the fact that it was late at night and that he had climbed into bed. If you have that kind of friend you don't really need enemies. What will you have to tell that friend in order for him to come out of his bed to render you help? Would you have to fabricate long-winded stories? Would you have to paint a picture of absolute misery in order to stir his sympathy? Perhaps you break down his door in frustration?

Our understanding of human friendship causes us to approach a friend when we are in need, and expect that the friend will do all he can to be of help.

> **If you treat this as a teaching based on comparison, and casually overcome the barrier placed there by Luke concerning friendship, you will end up painting God in a bad light.**

Those who hold the view that the parable is a direct representation of prayer automatically assume that the friend who would not come down because it was bedtime was God. In that scenario God might initially tell us that he is uninterested in our cause, but we are to persist. He is not easily entreated. The thinking is that after he has initially told us to go away, if we persist with pitiful tear jerking, and impossible sounding stories we are able to get some sympathy from God. Luke is forcing us to ask ourselves, is this fellow who is in bed really a friend?

The answer should really be a resounding no!

I don't think any of us will keep that kind of friend. We can trust our true friends, in spite of their human faults and weaknesses to come to our aid in time of need. The thought might run through their minds that they are tired, but most human beings will still get up to answer a friend.

Take note that the fellow making this request is not after a gift, he wants a loan! This friendship is a most adversarial one.

> **This cannot be a direct representation of what prayer is. We do not approach God asking for a loan! We don't go to God to lend us anything. Prayer is not a loan repayment scheme setup by God. We go to him because he is a giver.**

God's point communicated through Luke's writing style is that if we can trust our friends who are limited in resources, who sometimes are on a short emotional fuse and imperfect in character to come to our rescue, how much more dependable should our faith in a loving God who is ready to use his power on our behalf be?

If friendship will make a friend respond favourably to us, what would God do whose relationship with us is that of Father?

Jesus had just taught them to say, "Our Father who hath in heaven." He is now showing them how willing God our heavenly father is to show us his lovingkindness. He is Jehovah, the able and willing one. Luke's point is exactly the opposite of what that friend did. We don't have to hound God because God is not like that friend who stays in bed for selfish reasons. The point is that there is a quality of love in God that is so many-sided and ready to do us good such that no friendship can ever match it. God does not grumble, whine and complain when responding to you in prayer. God will not be rude to you for love is not rude. We can completely trust the unfailing mercy of our heavenly Father.

The conclusions are different depending on whether you receive the parable as a contrast or as a direct representation. The intended truth is realised when we treat this as a parable of contrast as it is with most of Luke's parables. Therefore draw confidence from the fact that God is good even when it is not immediately obvious. Do not be afraid to tackle the reality of evil and the perplexities of daily living but realise that your adventure into truth is exciting when you know that in God there is no iota of duplicity.

2

Why Parables?

34 All these things spake Jesus unto the
multitude in parables; and without a parable
spake he not unto them:

35 That it might be fulfilled which was
spoken by the prophet, saying, I will open my
mouth in parables; I will utter things which
have been kept secret from the foundation of
the world.

Matthew 13:34-35 (KJV)

Matthew tells us that every time Jesus taught the multitude, he spoke
parables unto them. So we know that whether the bible records it or
not, whenever Jesus ministered to the multitudes, he spoke a parable.
There are instances when these parables have been recorded for our
benefit and other times when these have not been recorded.

Jesus was speaking about things that had been shrouded in mystery
since the foundation of the world. These things that had been shrouded
in mystery from the foundation of the world remained so only because

no man had appeared on the scene that would utter them. If we are not careful, we will conclude that whatever has been concealed since the foundation of the world remains concealed because God wants them to remain hidden. The revelation of secret things requires men who are willing to declare them on earth. Jesus was the first man to open his mouth to make spiritual riddles understandable. During the public ministry of Jesus, God had found a man that he could use to reveal many secret things.

God reveals things but he is not a magician. He is limited to reveal as far as there is a man that utters God's truths.

Jesus used parables a lot in his earthly ministry. He used them to communicate profound spiritual truths.

And the disciples came, and said unto him,
Why speakest thou unto them in parables?
Matthew 13:10 (KJV)

The bible is not against us asking questions. Religion forbids it, but God permits it, encourages it and responds to our questions when we ask knowing that he is a God that reveals. From the nature of their questions, we can work out that the disciples did not praise Jesus for using parables. They were baffled that he used them so much even when the meaning was not obvious.

The nature of their query shows that His use of parables did not go down well with his audience, especially his disciples. It was obvious to the disciples that the multitude did not understand the parables. Truth be told the disciples also did not understand them. They did not understand the parable of the sower even after Jesus had told it so masterfully. He had to explain it to them in private! (See Matthew 13:18)

You see, even after Jesus, the master storyteller, had spoken to the multitudes in parables, it was still not granted unto them to understand the mysteries contained within them.

Contrary to popular belief, parables did not make it any easier to understand spiritual truth in Jesus' ministry.

The disciples only understood the parable after Jesus' explanation while the multitude remained in the dark. Let's see some scriptural references concerning parables.

> I will open my mouth in a parable: I will
> utter dark sayings of old:
> Psalm 78:2 (KJV)

David considered parables to be dark sayings of old. David was not isolated in this view; we see a similar idea presented in the inspired writings of the Prophet Ezekiel.

> Son of man, put forth a riddle, and speak a
> parable unto the house of Israel.
> Ezekiel 17:2 (KJV)

God, through the ministry of the Prophet Ezekiel admitted that parables were actually spiritual riddles. Ezekiel called them riddles while David called them dark sayings!

At face value it would seem that parables are simply stated earthly stories conveying spiritual realities that the simple should grasp. The weight of scripture however presents a different picture. The disciples' reaction tells us the exact opposite! Parables are difficult stories that are hard to understand.

Parables can be confusing. They require a lot more explanation before understanding can be extracted from them and even then, only a particular type of person grasps it.

> And he said, Unto you it is given to know
> the mysteries of the kingdom of God: but to

others in parables; that seeing they

might not see, and hearing they might

not understand. Luke 8:10 (KJV)

When Jesus said that it was given unto the disciples to know the mysteries of the kingdom of God, we need to realize that it was not given unto them to understand because they were officials per se but because they believed the word of Jesus. It is belief in Jesus that gives us the keys into the house of revelation knowledge. The others spoken of here are those who come to listen to Jesus but do not believe him.

> **Believing Jesus is the key that unlocks the understanding contained within the parables.**

Jesus is therefore saying that parables lock the unbelieving in a place where they have lack of understanding because they have closed their own eyes through willful unbelief.

> **Parables therefore are dark sayings that have different effects on the hearer depending on whether the hearer is a believing one or one who is embalmed in unbelief.**

We are forever grateful that the disciples asked this question. One thing that is obvious in scriptures is that spiritually intelligent people often ask questions while carnal people function by assumptions while all the while acting like they know what they are really ignorant of. When His disciples asked him why he spoke in parables, He answered by quoting Isaiah's sixth chapter.

Matthew was inspired to restate Isaiah in a way that conveys the truth more clearly.

> 14 And in them is fulfilled the prophecy of Esaias, which saith, By hearing ye shall hear, and shall not understand; and seeing ye shall see, and shall not perceive:
> 15 For this people's heart is waxed gross, and their ears are dull of hearing, and their eyes they have closed; lest at any time they should see with their eyes and hear with their ears, and should understand with their heart, and should be converted, and I should heal them.
> Matthew 13:14-15 (KJV)

The people qualified themselves for Isaiah's prophecy by allowing their own heart to become increasingly duller spiritually speaking.

The prophecy only applies to those type of people. Their eyes were closed to spiritual truth. Why was this the case? Who closed their eyes? Matthew gives us a key - God did not close their eyes, they did.

Do you know that you determine which prophecy will be fulfilled in your life?

The trigger was the people's heart, which became increasingly duller spiritually speaking. Do you know there is such a thing as retarding spiritually?

Jesus does not say: "In you all is fulfilled the prophecy of prophet Isaiah." He said "*in them*" is fulfilled the prophecy. He was speaking to his disciples and he implies his disciples were not in that group. The "them" is a reference to the people whose heart had waxed dull spiritually speaking. I never want this prophecy of Isaiah to be fulfilled in my life. I want to remain spiritually sharp! Exercising yourself in faith is good spiritual exercise in the gym of the word.

If you read Isaiah's record in the Old Testament it is not immediately obvious that the people were responsible for their own spiritual dullness. Matthew beautifully and faithfully records the Lord Jesus' quotation of Isaiah. In Jesus' quote, we receive further light that it was the people that closed their own eyes.

15

God did not close their eyes, they did. This means that they rejected the little light that they had for starters.

If we are not careful we read Isaiah's rendition, fill in the blanks and come away blaming God for the people's spiritual dullness.

> Ever learning, and never able to come to
> the knowledge of the truth.
> 2 Timothy 3:7 (KJV)

Just as in the ministry of Jesus, there are some that reject the light of God's word in Paul's ministry. When people do this, they are choosing to lock themselves into a place of spiritual blindness and ignorance. Since Paul accuses these people of ever learning but not coming of to the knowledge of the truth, it must mean that man has a principal part to play in coming to the knowledge of the truth.

You determine, to a large extend, how far you will go in developing spiritual intelligence. It is not God that determines whether men will understand the truth or not, it is within the sphere of man's authority. Those who have ears to ear progress into further understanding of truth while those who persist in unbelief close the door of revelation knowledge on themselves. We can say that the seed of God's word is always good but the soil of the human heart is the reason for variation in understanding or lack of it.

When the word is sent forth, it carries light that dispels darkness, but that light might be rejected or received. For those who receive it, they gain fresh insight and new understanding. For those who reject it, they remain blind and ignorant.

> **A parable therefore allows people to reap the condition of their heart. Hidden things remain hidden to those who reject truth, while they become knowledge and insight to those who have ears to hear.**

Whenever people start rejecting the truth, they put themselves in a position where they become dull to spiritual truth. This set of people cannot benefit from a parable for the parable only amplifies their confusion.

> **The parable did not confuse them, they were confused already but just did not know it.**

The parable merely amplifies the confusion that the hearers already had when they chose to reject the truth. As far as we can tell from the bible records, Jesus only ever explained the parables to his disciples, never to the multitude in whose presence it was spoken.

34 All these things spake Jesus unto the
multitude in parables; and without a parable
spake he not unto them:

Matthew 13:34 (KJV)

At some point in his ministry, Jesus resorted to the use of parables. We know that whenever Jesus faced a multitude he used parables extensively. Most of his parables are not recorded but we can learn a lot from the ones that we have on record.

Jesus did not stop using parables because his disciples pointed out that the multitudes were not getting it. Parables hide understanding from the unbelieving one while serving as a bridge of understanding to those that believe. The key is not the parable itself but the condition of the heart of the hearer. Parables are not magical teaching mechanisms that unmask spiritual truths in and of themselves. If we go by the disciples' reaction to Jesus' use of parables, we have to conclude that parables do not make it any easier to understand spiritual truth except the one hearing the truth is meek.

If we are going to be scriptural about it, based on the evidence from Jesus ministry when he used parables, we have to abandon the idea that parables teach spiritual truths so that even a fool can understand them. That is not what we see from the evidence of scripture and if we are open to accept it that is not the evidence we see from experience either. If anything, parables selectively open a door of understanding for those whose hearts are ready for truth, while permitting those who reject the light of God's word to remain outside the sphere of revelation knowledge. A parable is therefore a double-edged sword. The parable clearly aids ease of recall but does not necessarily increase understanding.

We know for a fact that for those that persist in unbelief a parable also aids easy recall but does nothing to progress their understanding of truth.

> 52 Woe unto you, lawyers! for ye have taken away the key of knowledge: ye entered not in yourselves, and them that were entering in ye hindered.
> 53 And as he said these things unto them, the scribes and the Pharisees began to urge him vehemently, and to provoke him to speak of many things:
> 54 Laying wait for him, and seeking to catch something out of his mouth, that they might accuse him.
> Luke 11:52-54 (KJV)

Perhaps another reason why Jesus used parables extensively was because there were evil people examining every statement of Jesus with the intention of finding grounds for arresting him. Jesus' use of parables made their task supremely difficult. You cannot arrest a man who tells stories!

Parables allow spiritual truth to remain hidden from view of those who persist in unbelief while presenting a mechanism for the ready heart to receive further light. A parable always requires explanation before understanding comes forth.

3

The Characters in the Parable

And he spake a parable unto them to this
end, that men ought always to pray, and not
to faint;

Luke 18:1 (KJV)

A parable is a spiritual story illustrating deep truths for the benefit of
those who believe. A parable is allegorical. Hidden within the story is
the message. Therefore parables need to be explained in order to draw
benefit.

Think of a parable as a portable way of transporting the understanding
of truth. Jesus told the stories to engage the attention of his believing
hearers.

Jesus had to use parables because even though these folks
sought to believe him, there was a limitation on what they
could understand in that day because they had not received
eternal life.

Their spirits were not yet reborn therefore their level of spiritual comprehension was limited.

I cannot imagine the Father God talking in parables to the Holy Spirit. When two equals are conversing, there is absolutely no need for a parable. Whenever there is a wide knowledge gap, parables can be used to bridge the gap. Even then, a parable does not guarantee that understanding will take place. Parables only help those that approach with a believing heart. Parables convey nothing to the unbelieving one. According to Jesus, a parable hides truths from the unbelieving.

> **Faith must be present before parables can serve their purpose as suitcases of understanding.**

When we were younger they told us many stories using the animal kingdom, but none of those stories were really about animals. The aim was not to make us zoologists. The story-tellers were communicating beautiful lessons of life in palatable language.

This parable of Jesus illustrates that if we don't pray we faint more easily. It unlocks for our attention: the anatomy of fainting, spiritually speaking, and what happens when we don't faint. If we faint long enough, we stop praying. If we pray extensively we stop fainting. This is because spiritual communion gets us built up on our most holy faith.

We only faint because we abandoned our God-consciousness. The first seven verses of Luke 18 completely communicate a full thought.

The granddaddy of all parables is the parable of the sower for in it he gave us the fundamentals for activating God's kingdom.

> **From this parable, we understand that the word of God is seed and it must be planted into the human heart, in order to release its power.**

This woman is doing some planting. She also does some reaping. Unlike the parable of the sower, Jesus did not explain this parable of the unjust judge in detail.

> Saying, A certain judge there was in a certain city. God he did not fear, and man he did not respect. Now, there was a widow in that city, and she kept on coming to him at recurring intervals, saying, Protect me by an equitable administration of justice from my opponent in a lawsuit...
> Luke 18:2-3 (Wuest)

The major characters are a judge, a widow, and her adversary.

She came to him saying Luke 18:3b (KJV)

What was this woman saying to that judge? She was speaking the gospel. The gospel is the power of God. The power in the word was delivered to this woman when she came in contact with the word. Everywhere she went she carried that power within her. This power needed to be released through her words and poured out into something.

This widow approached the judge with her words. When you speak, you are approaching something. She was in control of what to say. It was not up to the judge or the adversary. She was supplying the word of God, which is the power of God to bring about something favorable in that situation. In a sense you could also say that she was in control of how much power to release to bring about desired change.

This widow could point to a specific period of conscious release of words, a time when she decided to speak to the unjust judge. It is good to generally use our words scripturally, but there is something about setting time aside to speak the truths of God's word. You could locate exactly what this widow wanted.

The unjust judge did not scratch his head wondering what the widow intended. She knew what she wanted. He knew what she wanted.

She was not full of unnecessary stories. She did not approach him with her story; she came with clearly stated desire. She was lucid.

> **You can listen to many Christians talk for hours and you are no clearer at the end of the conversation than you were at the onset. They say a lot, but there is a lot of heat but little light in their words.**

Our thoughts are to be clear. Our words are to be unambiguous, lucid, crisp and full of light.

A clearly stated desire has the power to trouble the judge.

When she approached the unjust judge we are not told that she went bawling and squalling. We are not even told the specifics of the injustices that she must have suffered. We are not told that she even recounted this to the judge when she approached him in her words. The secret of this widow was that she was calling forth the end result. She filled her heart with a clear expectation, an inner image of how things should turn out and poured those expectations out as spoken words.

This woman came asking to be avenged of her enemies. She would not allow herself the luxury of playing the victim. She was willing to hold the adversary accountable for his actions. There is something of the spirit of a warrior about her.

Jesus borrowed from the legal system. In the court, you don't sway the judge by tears. You make a judge decide in your favour by your arguments and the lucidity of your presentation. You do not leave it to chance, happenstance, lady luck or fate.

> **When you want to enforce change in your world, don't try tears of despair. If all the tears that were shed on this earth would have swayed power away from the oppressors, there should be no power on the side of the adversary today.**

Someone is crying in some corner of the world today because life has not dealt a favorable hand. The tears don't change things. I think the tear glands are best utilized when we saturate our soul with the inner image of our desires.

It is good to get all emotional about God's word.

Imagine walking up to a friend who is just blabbing and tears are flowing like a fountain. When you finally ask the friend the reason for the tears and you hear the response, "I am emotional because I have seen my victory though my hands have not touched it yet". Tears are therapeutic when victory is sure within. At the very worst cry because you have the manifest victory.

> Avenge me of my adversary...
> Luke 18:3c (KJV)

We learn a valuable fact, from this parable, that an adversary should not be ignored. If your adversary challenges you to court and you agree with their estimation of you, you should not be surprised if you lose the case.

Just as the woman told the judge her expected outcome, we are to educate the judge and use our words to influence what decision we want the judge to arrive at. You are to say the word to your judge until your judge is saturated with truths from the celestial city. The judge will begin to judge righteous judgments.

The widow took a stand and by her words she approached the judge. She believed that by her words she could receive outcomes that were completely different from what the adversary was plotting. She was not a victim. This was one warrior of a woman!

This woman had an adversary and she knew it. She knew her troubles involved the activities of the adversary. She did not spend all her time grappling with the adversary.

> **We learn from Jesus' portrayal of this woman that lasting change does not come about by speaking to the adversary all day long. Watch who you spend all your time talking to because after a while you might start sounding like them!**

Find out what the word says and make it your continual confession. Then continuing to act on the word will bring God's will to pass. We learn from her that we should never abandon that which we know to be the truth.

> 2 Saying, A certain judge there was in a certain city. God he did not fear, and man he did not respect. 4 And he kept on being unwilling to do so for a considerable time.
> Luke 18:2,4 (Wuest)

When the widow first approached this judge, he had no intention of helping her. He would not for a while. The mood is that of one who kept on being unwilling to exercise justice. While he takes his time the city is under the grip of the adversary. This is a formidable judge. His unfavorable, cold and detached disposition would have been obvious to this widow. It would stop any other widow but not this woman.

The indifference of the unjust judge would have been the number one reason why this woman would have given up.

> **This is the single greatest reason why people faint, the indifference of the judge.**

How do we change the stance of the unjust judge?

We change the stance of the unjust judge by what we say. We know this judge can be made to change his stance, so we arm ourselves with that consciousness. The things that we say are facts that are based on the legal books.

This woman was not led by the reaction of the unjust judge. Perhaps she could make out that the unjust judge did not really care about her cause or her welfare. She is commendable in that she focused on speaking the word. She did not get bitter, twisted or distracted. She must have known the credentials of God's word and its ability to prevail in any situation.

> Yet, because this widow troubleth me... lest
> she weary me.
> Luke 18:5 (KJV)

It is interesting to note the effect that this widow's words were having on the judge. The judge did not really tell her that her words were troubling him, but they were. She did not necessarily know the effect she was having on the judge. She knew that by her words she was painting the picture of the desired outcome.

Jesus, by this parable gives us insight into the way the affairs of the earth are run.

You do not get what is due to you just because you deserve it. You don't assume that others ought to know what is yours by right. You present your case. Some people are forever perplexed wondering why things have not turned out the way that they assumed it was going to turn out. They feel cheated and wonder why things appear to go on unperturbed around them. In their minds, they wonder if God really cares. They respond to hopelessness and allow their fire to go out.

Solomon observed the state of play in his day and made the following observation.

9 How long wilt thou sleep, O sluggard? when wilt thou arise out of thy sleep?
10 Yet a little sleep, a little slumber, a little folding of the hands to sleep:

11 So shall thy poverty come as one that travelleth, and thy want as an armed man.

Proverbs 6:9-11 (KJV)

Some are forever folding their hands, waiting for God to do something. They think this is deep piety and profound spirituality. Solomon was inspired to call it the way of the sluggard!

> **They are hoping that God will do something, and God is hoping they would do something. They think that they are waiting on God, all the while God was waiting on them to stir out of sleep. Interestingly God gives us more latitude to act than we give him credit for.**

There is a time to arise from sleep and inertia otherwise we empower poverty to rob us of the blessing of God. Poverty is a thief that has been let loose on the earth. It is forever travelling, in perpetual motion seeking the sluggard in whose life he can build his kingdom. In simple terms, roll up your sleeves and let God's word stir you to action!

> **Ordered action spectacularly limits the devil. Things don't happen to us just because we are waiting.**

If you do nothing, you actually don't reap anything; you reap reduction and not increase. Why is this so? From the bible, we know it is so because of the laws of sin and death that Adam has released into this earth. The earth works the way it does because of the choices made by Adam. These choices have then been enforced by the unrenewed mind in every generation since Adam.

The city is a picture of the earth. This city that the widow lived in was not a neutral state of affairs. The fact that something is yours by right does not mean that it will come to you on a platter of gold.

A judge is reactive. He needs something to react to. A judge is also someone who listens to all sides on a matter before arriving at a decision. If there are no facts presented, there is no raw material for the judge to use to deliver judgment.

The judgment that the widow was seeking was to render the adversary ineffective and to swing the balance of power in favour of the widow. From the interaction between the widow and the judge, we gain insight into one of the reasons why we confess the word.

Why does the Christian confess God's word?

From this parable, one reason why we confess the word is to trigger favourable judgment in line with what God has said in his word already.

Our confession affects the unjust judge and troubles him to deliver the judgment that we desire. This triggers the manifestation of our rights.

> **You are not really confessing the word of God in order to change God or the adversary. You do not really want God to change. He is good. You are confessing God's word in order to set the boundaries of judgment and to establish cornerstones.**

In all of this, you must remember that this widow is coming to an unjust judge who sees her in cold and detached terms. The widow is not related to the unjust judge. The unjust judge does not care about her. Things don't look right in that city. Even when things don't look right, this widow is able to get things in her favour.

The widow's actions represent the action of those who believe God in the face of adversity in a fallen world. We have union with Christ who is seated at the right hand of God but we find ourselves in a fallen world. We make it our duty to bring the atmosphere of heaven into our world.

As a believer you must realize that the adversary is not the one that determines your outcomes in life. His roar does not determine what shall be. The future does not belong to him as much as he wants you to believe. The desired deliverance is often aborted because of thinking and believing wrongly about man, the devil and God. Together with this woman we do not think or believe that the adversary has the last say.

> **Many Christians unconsciously think that God is responsible for the evil that goes on in their world. Some are less in your face about it, so they say that God does not really cause it, he only permits it.**

Through this parable we have been given a glimpse of the enemy, and he is not God. The adversary is satan, the diabolic one, who seeks opportunities to devour (See 1 Peter 5:8). This widow knows that the adversary is the aggressor.

> **If you cannot distinguish between the work of the adversary and the work of God, your belief system will cause you to fold your arms and accept as your fate activities that are man-made supposing that they are God-ordained.**

We are authorised to find out God's will and to take a stand against anything that is remotely opposite to the known will of God. Since the widow came seeking judgment against the adversary, we can conclude that the adversary was clearly at work in that city. The widow also went to work with her words because she knows that the adversary is not the judge, and that he is only looking for those that will allow him to function as one.

Very often when we start out in life, we accept the status quo of the city. We think things happen because God has willed it so. The ideas of carnal people and those of the adversary, the devil, are very much the same so the poisonous ideas and false reasoning of the adversary go unchallenged. In that state we are unable to prove the will of God because we do not have any counter reasoning enforced through the word of God.

A believer must first awaken to the fact that getting run roughshod over is not the status quo in God and that it is not up to God to do something about it. We are to rise up with a consciousness that the tide of life can be turned through words that shape our actions. These words are to be directed primarily at the unjust judge.

> **The startling implication of the parable of the unjust judge is that the world continues as it is today because people permit it by losing courage when the outcomes they anticipate do not manifest as quickly as they thought it would.**

There are many things that God has disallowed that we consciously or unwittingly permit when we do not rise up like the widow and use the word of God to enforce the peace of God in any situation. Indecision is costly. The wicked and their crew are often more decisive in their pursuits than the righteous ones of God. This creates anarchy on earth.

> **It is really worth noting that the majority of the decisions that govern the world today are made and enforced by men functioning with an unrenewed mind. This is where the adversary gets his confidence, authority and influence.**

So get rid of all uncleanness and the rampant outgrowth of wickedness, and in a humble (gentle, modest) spirit receive and welcome the Word which implanted and rooted [in your hearts] contains the power to save your souls.
James 1.21 (Amplified)

This was written by James to Christians, therefore we know that once born again, the greatest need of the Christian is to get his soul saved. The soul does not get saved at the new birth. The new birth is a totally new creation of the human spirit.

Think about this carefully. The word of God has power to save the soul. Since this is the truth, you cannot pray more power into your life than that which can be made available through the word of God.

Start with the word and prayer makes sense

Prayer can make this power more perceptible or tangible to the touch but it does not present more power than is available through the word. Failing to recognise that it is the word that contains this power, we place more emphasis on who ministers the word than we do on the word itself. The word is the greater power. The minister conveys it. As you grow spiritually you come to place more emphasis on the word contained within a minister's delivery than on the minister himself. We bless God for ministers but the minister is not the answer. The word is. A good minister gets you to appreciate the word more.

> No word of God shall be void of power.
> Luke 1:37 (KJV)

Contained within every word of God is the power of fulfilment. This means that when God says something, the very word spoken has within it the power to bring itself to pass. However this power remains within the word until released by someone that believes. Though the word of God is full of power, the power within the word of God is not released of its own accord until we act on it. This is because the word of God operates like a seed. Things just don't change of their own accord because of the power of God's word.

You are authorised to locate the word concerning a situation and when you do, you are to act like someone who has found the power to change the facts of that situation to conform to the truth of God.

Zero Assumptions

> And having thrown off his outer garment,
> having leaped up, he came to Jesus...
> Mark 10:50 (Wuest)

In the ancient world, very much like our present day, you can tell a person's social standing and function by their clothing. It is symbolic that the blind man cast away his garment. The garment likely identified him as a beggar in that day. I don't think it was just a case of others seeing him as a beggar, he also thought of himself as one and his clothing left no one in doubt about it. There is a strong relationship between the state of the mind and the way we dress. I believe that when this blind man cast away that garment, he climbed up the ladder of life. Something within him had caught onto new outcomes. He was going to be a blind beggar no more!

Here is a blind man, who up till that time was a functional beggar, following hard after Jesus. The devil's gangs were there in huge numbers, and they were present to shut him up and kill his hope. He is going against the mob culture. They are screaming at him. He is raising his voice above their noise. All this while Jesus just kept walking on! He only stops when he enters a house. This crying, screaming, ridiculed but courageous blind man kept following Jesus, and he was still blind.

Jesus enters a house and then asks the blind man, "What do you want me to do?" This kind of question messes up the religious mind. If any man of God asks a struggling, tearful, blind man what he desired today, there are many people that will quickly consider that minister a charlatan.

We conclude that a crying blind man must surely want to receive the opening of his sight. Jesus does not assume. He asks. The blind then had the opportunity to state what we assumed to be obvious.

The truth is that no matter how obvious things seem, spiritually speaking, until voiced, we don't set ourselves in the position to receive.

And it shall come to pass, if thou shalt hearken diligently unto the voice of the

LORD thy God, to observe and to do all his
commandments which I command thee this
day, that the LORD thy God will set thee on
high above all nations of the earth:
2 And all these blessings shall come on thee,
and overtake thee, if thou shalt hearken unto
the voice of the LORD thy God

Deuteronomy 28:1-2 (KJV)

The key words are the words hearken, and diligent. That word translated as hearken means to hear intelligently and declare, while the word translated diligently there means completely, wholly, fast, louder and louder. The woman in the parable of the widow did not appear before the judge assuming that the judge knew her desires. She did not leave it up to that judge to figure it out. Our words are designed to express our will.

And He was giving them an illustration
which had for its teaching point that it is a
necessity in the nature of the case for them at
all times to be praying and not to be losing
courage;

Luke 18:1 (Wuest)

Kenneth Wuest's translation brings out the fact that it takes courage to pray. Prayer sustains courage and courage feeds prayer. When Jesus said that men ought always to pray, did he mean for us to interpret this as saying that day and night we are to be making requests to God? If we apply the traditional ideas about prayer to this, we come away thinking that making requests to God is what we should do all day and all night. Literally you could do that and die having received nothing.

To continue to be relevant and functional on earth, there are many things that the word of God instructs us to do. We are told to work with our hands that which is good, we are told to sleep after our daily work, we are told to rejoice no matter what and we are even told to give a cup of drink to a brother in the name of the Lord. If all we do is go on our knees and make requests to God day and night, we make the word contradict itself because many other things are left undone.

I am convinced that he was adjusting our understanding of what constitutes prayer. He means that all that we do through the day should be done in the understanding that the most mundane of actions should be a conversation with God.

In as much as you are doing all things in the name of Jesus, every action is a conversation with the word. I take this to teach that we are to live in a continuous communion with God whether a request to

God is involved or not. When Luke refers to ceaseless prayer, he is teaching us about a persistent and functional God-consciousness.

4

Identifying the Adversary

In this parable, Jesus does not tell us a lot about what the adversary said or how he operates for that matter. We do know that the adversary was the reason why this widow approached the judge. The widow wanted to be avenged of her adversary who was contrary to her. The judge was going to deliver the sentence.

Though we do not find any words on the lips of the adversary, we know that the widow felt his activities. The adversary loves to hide wherever possible. It is commendable that this widow was able to distinguish between the judge and the adversary.

What is clear in this parable is that the adversary is not the judge though he is trying to pass himself off as one.

Can we identify this adversary?

That is an innocent sounding question until you plumb the scriptures. Adam's fall sprung from the fact that he mistrusted God. He effectively saw God as an adversary. He could not accept that God had his best interest at heart. The fallen mind sees God as an adversary that is worshipped so as to be appeased.

When questioned as to why he sinned, Adam's response was "its the woman you gave me." As far as we can tell, Adam was the first being on record to blame God, as the source of his misfortune. In other words, Adam is saying, "God, the woman that you gave me has done to me what you permitted her to do," She definitely caused it while you permitted it. Adam believed that both Eve and God had ganged up against him to bring about his fall.

> **An interesting hallmark of the religious mind through the ages is that everyone born of Adam modifies this initial accusation. Some have found brilliant ways of wrapping that original accusation in religious speak but the key idea, lingering in the human psyche, is that God is our adversary.**

Contrary to religious propaganda, God was not the one that tempted Adam to sin. We know this because James gives us valuable insight.

> But each one is being solicited to sin when
> he is taken in tow and enticed by his own
> craving. Then, when the aforementioned

craving has conceived, it gives birth to sin,
and this sin when it is full grown brings
forth death...

James 1:14-15 (Wuest)

Death has been in the lineage of man for millennia, but no explanation of the type that James gives here were attempted in the Old Testament. This is the explanation of the events that played out in the Garden of Eden. We are forever grateful that Pastor James lifts the curtain and shows us the mechanics of temptation. Temptations are only as effective as the cravings that we permit in our heart. The temptations that we are exposed to, draw their power from the intensity of our desire.

> **Where there is zero desire, the tempter, whoever he may be, is guaranteed to fail. You cannot be tempted beyond what your thought will permit. One cannot help but wonder if Jesus ever faced temptation of the sort that James describes here.**

Temptation uses our lusts to draw us away. "Away from what?" you may ask. Temptations draw us away from the word.

Let no man say when he is tempted, I am
tempted of God: for God cannot be tempted

with evil, neither tempteth he any man:
James 1:13 (KJV)

When James says "Let no man say", we know that in context he is discussing the double-minded man from the sixth verse who is devoid of divine wisdom. This man, just like Adam, is especially double-minded about God. One minute he thinks God is good and the next he is convinced that God tempts with evil.

When tempted, Adam laid it at God's doorstep. Pastor James tells us that no man should use the language that Adam used. When we use the wrong words to describe God we feed ourselves with a wrong image concerning him. These images prevent us from seeing him for who he really is. We see a God that we have hidden behind layers of wrong religious thinking.

It is worthy of note that when we accept the wrong image about God, we setup ourselves to experience our false expectations of him. Religious tradition causes us to worship our own fears unconscious that God is altogether different. We are experiencing our own fears but are often unaware that this is the case.

Whatever you say about God, you open up yourself to experience.

This does not mean that God supports your ideas concerning him but he will bless you as far as he can because that is who he is. We mostly experience outcomes from the laws of reaping which are at work on the earth and all the while we are convinced that God is trying to determine our breaking point. This is delusion. We can recover from this delusion by guarding what we say in our heart about God. James teaches us that there is evil on earth but God and evil do not go hand in hand. God does not use evil to accomplish his purposes.

> **We learn from James that when our lusts come into agreement with the tempter, sin is conceived which leads to evil on earth.**

According to James, Man conceives the evil that we see on earth today. The mystery surrounding evil vaporizes when we get a scriptural introduction to man and his methods. He is double minded therefore unstable in his ways. Man prefers to sow to his flesh and from the flesh he reaps corruption. He also co-creates this delusion with a fallen angel who steals, kills and destroys.

> **Man has ganged up with satan over several millennia to co-create the trauma that we see on earth today. The earth manifests these traits of instability only because man is unstable and the devil is diabolical.**

7 Be subject with implicit obedience to God at once and once for all. Stand immovable against the onset of the devil and he will flee from you.

James 4:7 (KJV)

8 Be of a sober mind, be watchful. Your adversary who is a slanderer, namely, the devil, as a lion roaring in fierce hunger, is constantly walking about, always seeking someone to be devouring. Stand immovable against his onset, solid as a rock in your faith, knowing that the same kind of sufferings are being accomplished in your brotherhood which is in the world.

1 Pet 5.8-9 (Wuest)

No one can submit you to God, only you can. The kind of submission that the bible encourages flows from a quality decision to side in with God's word, even with your back against the wall.

We are not taught in the New Testament to submit to God and then all things magically get resolved around us. The fact is that while you may chose to submit to God, there are other people in your community who might choose not to submit themselves to God. When people do not submit to God, they are unconsciously submitted to the devil. We are to be rock solid in our faith-stand against the devil and he will do the fleeing.

While the current state of affairs persists on the earth, we are to submit to God while we resist the devil. Many people do one or the other. Start by submitting to God, when you know who God is, you know what he will do. This enables you to intelligently spot that which is not God. You then resist that which is not God. The adversary hides and only shows his hands in diabolical ways. When the adversary is at work it is often so easy to explain things away by pointing the finger at everyone else. Even though Adam was present when satan tempted Eve, he bluntly refused to consider that the serpent was his real enemy and not God. Satan's greatest trick is to remain as hidden as possible.

> "Hey Adam, why have things collapsed around you?"
>
> "Dude, its God. He is against me. Eve has joined in also."
>
> "Hey Eve, why have things collapsed around you?"
>
> "Dude, it's the devil."
>
> Eve was closer to the truth.

Anyone listening to that conversation will be confused! Adam and Eve could not even agree why their world collapsed. Adam and Eve are like many people today; they fail to see that they have a part to play in the game of life. They blame everyone else. They shift blame and continually play the victim. Tragically, there are so many well-meaning people that think that they are submitting to the will of God while in reality they are allowing their adversary to operate unhindered in their lives.

Time and again, we see that if we do not know what God is like, we will submit to the devil's works and attribute it to God. Many are left scratching their heads wondering why God has supposedly repaid them with evil when they had served him diligently.

Peter bails us out of this confusing loop by naming the adversary. The devil is the adversary. God is nowhere presented in the New Testament as our adversary. This knowledge should be an anchor for our soul and frees us from submitting, while assuming God is at work when we should be resisting. This resisting is in the faith. This means in the word. To resist steadfast in the faith means to resist consistent with what you believe to be true.

While the word of God is good weaponry in the midst of battle, it seems that the real intention of God is to use the word to stir in us a longing for battle way before it shows up on our doorstep. As we feed on the word, there is energized in us the readiness to stand forever if need be until our victory is manifest.

When you act as the adversary expects, you unconsciously cause him to gain confidence. We are not told to tell God to tell the adversary to leave us alone.

> **When God empowers us to resist the devil and we do not, we are permitting the devil's operations in our little corner of the world. People who do not resist the devil are prone to say God is permitting the devil's operations.**

In your Canaan, the old armies of doubt, fear, unbelief, and condemnation are trying to set up an ambush aimed at tricking you to release wrong confessions. Remember that you can combine the authority of spoken words and bold action to viciously decimate these enemies that war against your mind and emotions.

One of the clear images that we see in the Old Testament is that Jehovah is a victorious warrior. Since, we are his workmanship in Christ Jesus, we know that we carry the victorious warrior gene in our spiritual DNA. We don't give in, back down, let up, cave in or roll over. We savagely waste satan's works of unbelief, doubt, confusion and fear. We have submitted to God's ability and are assured of strength. Now we reach down into our spirit and run by God. (Zephaniah 3.17)

The pattern in the bible is that the natural first comes on the scene after which the stage is set for the spiritual fulfillment. This is true for the temple, the sacrifices, the Sabbath and many others. What do we make of Israel's violent wars in the Old Testament? Those wars transpired in the natural sphere of life. If we will accept it, the Bible records of the natural wars of Israel are an illustration of our spiritual war today. There is to be a brutality about us as we take a stand against the devil, his demons, their false philosophies and their intricate web of lies. Just as Ai was burnt down, there are whole systems of thinking that we must obliterate by the power of God's word.

Peter gives us insight into how to withstand the adversary.

The best ammunition for withstanding the adversary is the ammunition of a sober mind. Sober does not mean existing in a bland, lifeless and colorless state. The Greek word means to be safe in mind. This refers to soundness of mind. A sober person as used here is one who has self-control in emotion and action.

Your greatest weapon against the adversary is a strong mind as well as balanced emotions. If your mind is kept strong and your emotions enabled with the word, the adversary has no means of penetrating the hedge of protection in your life. People easily fall prey to the adversary during periods of mental weariness and emotional distress. Peter lends a hand here and peels back layers of confused thinking that has prevailed through the ages when he says that God should be submitted to while the devil should be resisted.

> **He is teaching that we don't accept everything that comes our way as our lot in life. Things happen in our lives that are not part of God's plan for us.**

When we see things that are contrary to God's nature happen in our lives, we are to identify that the adversary is at work and then resist him steadfastly. We now know that God is not our adversary. Peter's insight gives us the tools to unmask the religious mindset that encourages us to be double-minded about God's character. Peter's assertion sounds simple until you open the pages of your Bible and read some mind-boggling things attributed to God!

The teachings that school us into thinking of God as an adversary do not take place in the comfort of our homes; neither do they get propounded at night clubs and pubs. They fly at us during church services! This is because the way the Bible is written sometimes leaves the casual reader with the idea that God is adversarial. In time we speak enough Christianese to convince ourselves that he is a Father, but are unresolved in the light of these troubling verses of Old Testament scripture.

There is a reason why many people are unable to come to a clear picture as to whether an experience is from God or from the devil. They are unsure who the adversary really is. This is where scriptural thinking is tasked to the max. If the weird things that most religious people attribute to God were half true, you would have to conclude that he puts the devil out of business.

How do we reconcile these things?

> And it is this message which we have heard
> from Him and at present is ringing in our
> ears and we are bringing back tidings to
> you, that God as to His nature is light, and
> darkness in Him does not exist, not even one
> particle...
> 1 John 1:5 (Wuest)

I cannot tell you how many times I have glossed over this verse in my early days as a Christian. Here was the apostle John declaring in the most emphatic of terms that there was absolutely no darkness in God, not even a particle and I did not believe it. I thought that I knew of instances here and there where I could point to some form of darkness in God. While I sang well-known songs that spoke of the goodness of God, I really believed about God things that no one would believe about a good human being good human being, let alone a merciful God. This was because of my not rightly dividing the word and my refusal to harmonize various things different writers stated about God.

> **I used to think that God deals a good hand to me if I am compliant but that should I draw back from following his terms, he gets grieved, hides his face from me while conducting back-door negotiation with satan to bully me into submission to God.**

Based on the way I reasoned back then, satan's assignment from God was to ride roughshod over me until I agree that I should not have withdrawn from God in the first place.

When it is all reduced to basics, I really believed that God uses satan to keep me towing the straight and narrow road.

> **It is mind-boggling the traumatic mess that religion gets us to accept. How could I have believed that God and the devil were tag teaming to keep me straight!**

My understanding of troubling statements in the Bible was killing my comprehension of who God really was, but I did not immediately see it. I, who am declared to be God's own very epistle, was disregarding the light of life in my spirit. The spirit was trying to show me more but I had stumbled badly at the stone of literal reading.

Dear John, how you wound our fanciful thinking with truth! How could John say so emphatically that there was zero darkness in God in the light of what he must have read in the scriptures from Genesis through Malachi in that day?

The prevailing thought was that both darkness and light were attributable to God. John, like most had bought into this. Something happened to John though that caused him to state in the absolute negative that there is no darkness in God at all. There was something that had opened to him a door of understanding into another world. When John spoke of the message that we have heard, it was not that he had directly been to heaven to attend one of God's pastoral meetings.

> **He could speak in assured terms as to what God is like because he has seen and heard him in Jesus.**

After John had been exposed to the message of God in the life of Jesus, he came to an emphatic conclusion that there is no darkness in God at all.

> 9-10 "You've been with me all this time, Philip, and you still don't understand? To see me is to see the Father. So how can you ask, 'Where is the Father?' Don't you believe
>
> that I am in the Father and the Father is in me? The words that I speak to you aren't mere words. I don't just make them up on my own. The Father who resides in me crafts each word into a divine act.
> John 14:9-10 (The Message)

Jesus is the declaration of what God really is. It is safe to say that when I do see God, I perfectly expect him to be like the man Jesus in ethos, character and practice. Jesus has declared God not necessarily in physical appearance, but in manifesting his light, life and love.

Therefore we do ourselves a great favour paying close attention to Jesus. Whatever we do not find in Jesus is not true of God. Even when we think we can prove from the word that God is not love, we have simply found a verse that shows up our ignorance. The scriptures properly examined only prove that God's mercy is over all his works. Jesus as we see him in his earth walk is the full gospel. He is the greatest Bible exegesis.

Since we cannot conceive of Jesus as the ruler of darkness, we know that God is not the ruler of darkness. He is not the author of evil nor does he even permit any of these things. But ah! You say, "what of the myriad of scriptures that presents God as the one directly responsible?"This is uncomfortable territory for the religious mind. We must admit that any serious student of the word is forced at some time or the other to query whether the nature of God changed between the last words of prophet Malachi and that which we see demonstrated in the ministry of Jesus. What accounts for this contrast? A possible explanation is that in the Old Covenant, God had not revealed the adversary and his methods.

> **All those demons that were cast out in the earth walk of Jesus, what were they doing before Jesus came along? Why was there zero record of demons being cast out before the coming of Jesus? Clearly these demons were not idle bystanders. They were disruptive, but their actions would have been attributed to God!**

I am convinced that the reason why God appears to have changed between the Old Testament and the New Testament portrayal of him is because man's understanding of satan has changed. Both Man and satan have changed, but God remains the same.

> **Whatever man does not know about himself and satan, he readily attributes to God.**

You will discover as you read through the New testament that there is a progressive revelation of the part played by God, man and satan in the history of the earth. Naively in the early days, I had a fully developed understanding of satan gleaned from reading Genesis through Malachi.

I was in trouble because my beliefs did not allow for the fresh illumination available in the New Testament; I was Christian in name, but judaistic in thought and practice! I was at home with the idea that satan was doing the dirty work that forces man to make choices. I unconsciously saw him as acting under God's permission. I did not know what to do with Jesus' statement that satan was a thief with his own agenda of stealing, killing and destroying. He was acting without needing God's consent.

Jesus spoke of satan as an enemy and not as a servant of God. He said that when satan speaks the lie he is operating out of his own agenda as the father of lies. Moses never said this because Moses did not know. I was guilty of assuming that those precious Old Testament saints had access to New Covenant truth whereas they did not. I was uninformed about satan because my ideas about satan were well formed before I had even read what Jesus had to say about him as recorded in the gospels and later through his apostles in the epistles.

I was shocked the first time it dawned on me that Moses in all his writings never mentioned satan once!

Was this an omission? Moses was faithful. If he had light on the subject he would have written it. He was clueless about satan. I would be unfaithful to New Testament truth if I refused to harmonise my beliefs with the word.

In Old Testament times, even though the adversary, wicked men and other laws were actually responsible for evil acts, these were attributed to God. At other times the human element was discussed without reference to any spirit being's involvement. The collective consciousness of the people in the Bible was to attribute everything to the one that they know. In the ministry of Jesus, whatever we see Jesus do, that was God doing it. God has rescued our thinking. God had a vehicle for showing the operations that describe him as well as the operations of this adversary. What then is the explanation for the various things that were attributed to God in the Old Testament?

> 12 Not as Cain, who was of that wicked one,
> and slew his brother. And wherefore slew he
> him? Because his own works were evil, and
> his brother's righteous.
> 1 John 3.12 (KJV)

This is divine commentary on the events that transpired in the murder of Abel by Cain. The tragedy of premature death was as a result of the cooperation between Cain, a man, and the wicked one, satan the adversary.

The wicked one, the adversary, was active in that first murder but the Old Testament record of it was silent on the part played by the adversary. We now know that while the Old Testament is quiet on it, when Cain killed Abel he was under the influence of this wicked one, the adversary. If all that we had were the Genesis account, we would attribute the outcomes to everyone except the true adversary.

If anyone linked any spirit beings to Cain's actions back then, they are open to thinking that those spirits came from God. Some would even conclude that God permitted it. This is an example of the human element in the mystery of evil on the earth. Who permitted this evil? Cain directly permitted it and, to some extent Abel, who did not know how to obtain protection from God. Consider the puzzling piece of scripture below:

> 9 And the evil spirit from the Lord was upon
> Saul, as he sat in his house with his javelin in
> his hand: and David played with his hand.
> 1 Samuel 19.9 (KJV)

We are forced to ask, are there really evil spirits that come from God? Taken literally and at face value Samuel's record of events appears to say that God sent an evil spirit to torment Saul with some psychotic disorder and God then went across town and anointed David's music to drive the evil spirit away. If this were the case, then God's kingdom is against itself and cannot stand.

Saul had repeatedly sown to his flesh and his lack of confidence opened the door for demonic affliction. This demonic activity dismantled his psychological balance.

Concerning this supposed evil spirit that came from God to torment Saul, we have additional information from the bible.

And Saul's servants said unto him, Behold
now, an evil spirit from God troubleth thee.
1 Samuel 16:15 (KJV)

This sheds interesting light on the episode of the evil spirit from God.
Take particular note of the fact that this is something that Saul's
servants said unto him.

> **It would appear that the idea of evil spirits coming from God
> was the belief system of Saul's servant. It was the people's
> estimation of events in that day.**

These people were assuring Saul that these evil spirits were from God!
The people had a right to an opinion, but those opinions are not
necessarily true until examined in the fuller light of God's word.

Well, in the New Testament Jesus also sends evil spirits. He sends them
out of people. He cancels the influence of these demons over people.
Since Jesus is the clearest demonstration of whom God is and he sends
evil spirits out of people and we do not have any record of him sending
them into people in the Bible, we can safely conclude that God did
not send evil spirits to anyone. Consider another puzzling statement
below:.

> Again the anger of the LORD was aroused
>
> against Israel, and He moved David against
>
> them to say, "Go, number Israel and Judah".
>
> 2 Samuel 24:1 (KJV)

This is one of those statements in the Bible that seems to promote the idea that God is sometimes adversarial, but is he? The casual reader is forced to say that according to the way this text is written, it was the anger of the Lord that moved David to number Israel. Thus moved, David's action brought about the physical death of about 70,000 Jews. Did God inspire David to take this action? This is how the prophet Samuel recorded those events.

Those deaths were not due to some mystical wand waved in the sky by some being hungry for blood. While the death of those 70,000 was unnecessary, it is not as mysterious as it looks at first glance.

> 11-16 GOD spoke to Moses: "When you
>
> take a head count of the Israelites to keep
>
> track of them, all must pay an atonement-
>
> tax to GOD for their life at the time of being
>
> registered so that nothing bad will happen
>
> because of the registration. Everyone who

gets counted is to give a half-shekel (using the standard Sanctuary shekel of a fifth of an ounce to the shekel)—a half-shekel offering to GOD. Everyone counted, age twenty and up, is to make the offering to GOD. The rich are not to pay more nor the poor less than the half-shekel offering to GOD, the atonement-tax for your lives. Take the atonement-tax money from the Israelites and put it to the maintenance of the Tent of Meeting. It will be a memorial fund for the Israelites in honor of GOD, making atonement for your lives."

Exodus 30:11-16 (The Message)

The Exodus account gives us clarity from the word concerning Israel's conduct during any census. During the days of Moses, God had given clear instructions about the protocol for conducting a census. God's word already contained instructions on particular offerings to be presented before taking a census.

Conducting a census in and of itself is not an unholy thing. We know that census is not wrong because there is a book of the bible that derives its name from census results, the book of numbers! In choosing not to present the offerings, David exercised his will not to submit to

God's prescription. We find in scriptures, that if God is going to judge, he would warn the people first and give room for repentance.

> **Anytime you see random destruction involving the forces of nature, you must realize that these are not the operation of God but of the adversary.**

These are mostly due to the consequence of Adam's fall, the sinful actions of men, the operations of wicked spirits, or a combination of any of these factors, but never the signature of God. Now, before you draw any conclusions, have a look at how another bible writer who lived much later than Samuel records the exact same events leading up to David's census and the consequential deaths.

> Now Satan stood up against Israel, and moved
> David to number Israel. 2 And David said to
> Joab and to the rulers of the people, Go, number
> Israel from Beersheba even to Dan; and bring
> the number of them to me, that I may know it.
> 1 Chronicles 21:1 (KJV)

> **Between the record in Samuel and Chronicles, men had received more light on the operations on satan, the adversary.**

David's desire to conduct that census was not driven by anything pragmatic. First, David had the desire, this lustful desire became the adversary's open door to tempt David and induce him to sin and reap death. There were people like Joab, who were high-ranking officials around David, that pointed out to him the folly of his actions but he would not listen (1 Chronicles 21:3,6). He trusted in numbers rather than the help of the Lord. The census took almost a year (2 Sam 24.8). David therefore had ample time to repent, but repeatedly chose not to.

The writer of Chronicles says that it was satan that moved David to commit the sin, but in Samuel it says it was the Lord's anger, or His wrath. So which is it? Rest assured that there are no contradictions in God. One way of looking at this is that God usually restrained David from acting on his lusts but that this time around he did not stop David from responding to his own lusts. God could not stop David from reaping the harvest of his highly developed lustful desires. In that instance, David permitted satan to co-create the loss of human lives with him. That could be seen as God allowing it, in which case the language of Samuel should be permissive.

I am persuaded however that if God was allowing anything, he was allowing man to exercise his will. In this instance, as in most cases, man's will called upon a harvest of death. Whatever the case, we know that we must not interpret

Samuel as saying that God moved David. This is because God doesn't move people to sin.

Another fact we must not throw out the window is that God allowed the knowledge of the inspired writers to shine through. Many of the Old Testament writers lived without a knowledge of satan and his kingdom. All too often they projected satan's works unto God because they saw satan as an agent that could only act by God's permission.

> 13 Let no man say when he is tempted, I am tempted of God: for God cannot be tempted with evil, neither tempteth he any man:
>
> 14 But every man is tempted, when he is drawn away of his own lust, and enticed.
>
> 15 Then when lust hath conceived, it bringeth forth sin: and sin, when it is finished, bringeth forth death.
>
> James 1:13-15 (KJV)

The writings of James illuminate the record that we find in Chronicles and Samuel concerning the death of the seventy thousand Jews.

It would appear that David was drawn away by his own desire. This desire then opened the door for satan's provocation and

| **locked David in a vicious cycle of death.**

The more man enforces his own will, the less God is able to inject his mercy. When man turns his back to God's mercy by the exercise of his will against that which is known of God, the laws of sowing and reaping are unleashed. What Samuel recorded as the wrath of God is really the product of man reaping because he has sowed to his flesh.

This is not a case of God being personally angry towards David thereby triggering death; it was David triggering the process of death by his choices.

As further illustration, if I run a red light while driving, I would have set in motion events that could cause me to reap premature death. Exercising my will this way also abuses the will of other road users. My will has put both their lives and mine in danger. If they don't know how to respond to my madness, they might reap premature death. That is not God at work. It is foolishness and unlove cooperating with death.

24 Wherefore God also gave them up to uncleanness through the lusts of their own hearts, to dishonour their own bodies between themselves:

69

26 For this cause God gave them up unto vile affections: for even their women did change the natural use into that which is against nature:

Romans 1:24, 26 (KJV)

The Apostle Paul tells us that God does give people up to their vile affections. We little appreciate the devastating consequences of man's vile affections. This is man reaping where he has sown. So to speak, man is capable of wresting himself out of God's care. He inevitably reaps that which is devoid of mercy only because he has rejected the mercy of God at his disposal.

5 And he could there do no mighty work, save that he laid his hands upon a few sick folk, and healed them.

6 And he marvelled because of their unbelief. And he went round about the villages, teaching.

Mark 6:5-6 (KJV)

God was willing to do some mighty works in Jesus' hometown. The bible says that Jesus could not show mercy on a grand scale however much he tried. This religious village had mounted a blockade that hindered God's mercy. Whether we realise this principle or not, we do well to note that unbelief results in man taking sides against God's mercy while agreeing with the adversary who is a thief. In effect unbelief causes the works of the thief to remain unchallenged. It was God's mercy that sent Jesus to that town, but the collective unbelief of the people stopped him from achieving God's purpose. The people willed their problems to persist as they embraced unbelief. Their collective unbelief casted out the mercy of God! Jesus did not say God changed his mind. He said that it was their unbelief that caused that town to forfeit the mercy of God. The people through unbelief were not willing that the mercy of God be on display. This is the danger of unbelief - it causes us to depart from the mercy of God.

> 24 Another parable put he forth unto them, saying, The kingdom of heaven is likened unto a man which sowed good seed in his field:
>
> 25 But while men slept, his enemy came and sowed tares among the wheat, and went his way.
>
> 26 But when the blade was sprung up, and brought forth fruit, then appeared the tares also.
>
> 27 So the servants of the householder came

and said unto him, Sir, didst not thou sow

good seed in thy field? from whence then

hath it tares?

28 He said unto them, An enemy hath done

this.

Matthew 13:24-28a (KJV)

From the teachings of Jesus we understand that there is more than one source for the seeds that trigger harvests in nature as we understand it. We assume that it is God orchestrating events in the natural creation. The enemy also tries to plant effects through men that submit to him. We therefore understand that not all that happens around us is attributable to God.

> **We do not stop enough to ask, "These harvests of tsunamis, tornadoes, hurricanes and unmentionable disorders that we find in the bodies of men all over the earth, who is sowing these seeds?" We don't ask because we think we know. There is a tragedy worse than not knowing, it is the idea of thinking you know when you do not really know.**

When we do finally bring ourselves to ask, we phrase the question in unhealthy language. We say "Why does God permit evil?" That would be like picking up the tabloids and seeing the heading "Why did Princess Diana kill Abraham Lincoln?" What good could come out of that line of questioning?

The very question starts from the premise that God permits evil for reasons we don't know. God already stands accused. Perhaps we could rephrase it and be more investigative "Does God permit evil?" Couched in those terms, the picture changes and we are truly open to discover that according to Jesus "an enemy has done this." We are then left to investigate whether it was directly or indirectly. There are a lot of unnatural things, uncertainties and perplexities in nature but we are certain that the variation in our experiences is not down to some variation on God's part.

> **When life throws those random curveballs, we do well to remember that God only creates and initiates good.**

Every departure from God's plan in nature is either down tot he enemy, man or a partnership between the two of them. We can safely unmask the adversary in the parable of the unjust judge, it is that ancient serpent and deceiver.

5

Dark Sayings

And Saul's servants said unto him, Behold
now, an evil spirit from God troubleth thee.
1 Samuel 16:15 (KJV)

Saul's servants sought for explanations as to the cause of Saul's
psychological disorder and they came to a conclusion. They believed
believed that God sends evil spirits to trouble people. This was
their analysis. More light has been given to us today from the Holy
Scriptures than that which ever existed in the collective consciousness
of the people of the Old Covenant.

> **You don't read too far in the Old Testament scriptures before
> you come to the startling conclusion that the people who lived
> before the earth ministry of Jesus didn't know much about
> satan.**

There is neither instruction given on how to resist this adversary nor is
any insight given into the organisations behind his despicable operations.
This could explain why, in the Old Testament, sicknesses as well as the

evil spirits that tormented King Saul are said to come from God. This picture changes once you start reading the gospels and the accounts of the public ministry of Jesus. There is an explosion of references to satan, demons, evil spirits and the likes.

You start reading the gospels and once Jesus' public ministry starts there is an explosion of references to satan, demons, evil spirits and the likes. This same trend continued in the epistles.

> **Jesus was the dividing line. He was the marker from which we begin to see a constant revealing of satan's work and influence.**

Did the devil come alive during the earth walk of Jesus? Had he been dormant prior to that? So where was the devil in the Old Testament? Was the adversary waiting for Jesus to appear so he can start to manifest and mess with people?

The average believer that has heard biblical teaching about the realm of wicked spirits assumes that this mirrors the experience of the Old Testament saints. The truth is that the Old Testament writers did not bring forth much revelation concerning satan or demons. The whole of the Old Testament has just two direct references to demons while the New Testament usage of the same term is well over fifty. It was not that the population of demons multiplied in the New Testament or that the demons went to sleep in the Old Testament and came out of hibernation in the New. Little was written about them in the Old Testament because though present, their actions were seen as the judgement of God.

> **Jesus was the first human being on record to deal with the demons as adversaries. You will not find any record of Moses or any other Old Testament character casting out demons.**

Let us listen in to an imaginary conversation between Job and someone who has read the book of Job.

"Hey Job what's going on?"

"Well, the most high has been good to me in past times."

"Blessed be God. I don't see much of you these days though Job".

"Dear brother, it is because these days God is showing me his other side. He has sent evil my way so I will bear it in secret."

"Big man Job, what happened to your business?"

"Oh! You mean my livestock?"

"Yes Job."

"You see, my servants told me that the livestock market collapsed in an instant. They said that they saw lightings and fire from heaven burn up the sheep. Thus I know that God has sent me evil. He has taken back notion of satan. the livestock that he gave me. I will accept it.

There are mysterious things going on. My world is collapsing, but I accept the will of God. You won't believe half the things that have happened to me if I told you."

"I understand what you mean Brother Job. I have actually read your story."

"You did? Where did you come about my story?"

"There is a whole book of the bible dedicated to you, therefore, you must understand what I am saying about receiving good and evil from the Most High.

Well, brother Job from what I read, you are a commendable character. You are a good man. The writer of your story gave a glimpse as to what happened behind the curtains in the drama of your life. It was not God who was against you, it was satan."

Job laughs.

"You sound like that fellow Elihu who insisted that God would not afflict (Job 37.23). Pray tell brother, you speak funny and you propose strange ideas. Do you know how many times I let God know that I am receiving evil as part of his will? He had opportunity after opportunity to let me know if it was satan behind those losses and tragedies as you say but he did not. Put on sack cloth and ashes and repent for we know that this is God at work and not some silly notion of satan.

Don't read that casually. By God's admission, Job was a first class spiritual man of that time. He was top of the pyramid spiritually speaking. If that was Job's analysis of events of that day, what would others believe who are godless?

While the writer of the book of Job wrote by the revelation of God, Job himself did not know that it was satan that was against him. He thought he was receiving good and evil from God! Since they only knew about God, whenever anything supernatural would occur whether good or bad, they would often attribute it to God automatically because they just didn't know any better and their understanding was darkened. The veil was in various degrees and it was enforced by the near silence in the Old Testament.

> **They saw satan as just another angel of God, operating by His divine permission and direction.**

When Adam fell, he ushered in global consequences for all his progeny. Today, man grapples with the curses that were the consequences of the fall of Adam but he does not know it. that it is all part of God's original plan. Consider Job's experience once more:

> And the Lord said unto Satan, Behold, all that he hath is in thy power; only upon himself put not forth thine hand. So Satan went forth from the presence of the Lord. Job 1.12 (KJV)

> **You could tell what a man believes about God, satan and man by listening to him after he has tried to analyse the book of Job. Without a doubt the book of Job is a nightmare to most Christians.**

It is the only book in the Bible where God is holding conversations with the adversary. It is also an undeniable fact that the numbers three and seven play a pivotal role in this story. The pattern of threes and sevens occur just too many times. There were four recorded tragedies that befell Job and in each only one person escapes the tragedy to deliver the bad news to Job.

> **It is noteworthy that the contains the most references to satan in the whole of the Old Testament.**

The clearest description of the operation of the adversary is that which is recorded in the book of Job. Students of the Bible tell us that a better rendition of the Hebrew word, translated "satan" in the book of job, should be translated as adversary.

Right from the first chapter we can see that satan was the direct cause for Job's suffering. Since the book of Job contains information on the death of Job, it is likely that Job did not write the whole book or any of it. It is likely that God inspired someone other than Job to write these records. It is evident that Job did not know about the things that transpired in the first chapter.

Satan, as the adversary, incited God against Job by accusing Job before God.

> And the Lord said unto Satan, Hast thou
> considered my servant Job, that there is
> none like him in the earth, a perfect and an
> upright man, one that feareth God, and
> escheweth evil? Job 1:8 (KJV)

When God says to satan "have you considered my servant Job?", the thinking in most quarters is that God is drawing a name from the celestial lottery machine and suggesting to satan the next person to be bullied by satan. People assume that Job won this lottery with God's blessing.

I believe that this cannot be the case, but that in the light of the fact that God knows all things, God is simply exposing satan's thoughts back to satan. He is saying in effect "satan, knowing you and your methods, in your roamings on the earth you must have come across my servant Job and you are weighing him in the balances to find out how you might get to him."

> The whole world lies in the power of the evil
> one. 1 John 5:19 (KJV)

Job was not born again. As a partaker of spiritual death and one who by nature was a child of wrath he was under satan's jurisdiction already.

When God said that "all he has is in your power," was God handing Job over to satan? No. God was simply stating the facts. God was not handing Job over to satan the adversary, nor was he giving him information to put Job in trouble. The state of affairs without a redeemer was such that all that Job had was in satan's power.

> **When God said "do not put your hands on him" or "only spare his life," what was going on? It would appear that satan should have been able to touch everything that relates to Job, but that God's mercy was restricting satan.**

Perhaps if this conversation had not taken place, satan was going to waste Job's life. It was to Job's advantage that the conversation took place. The conversation limited satan as best as he could be limited until Jesus came. Job lived before the New Covenant was in force. We cannot have a New Testament Job because according to the Apostle John, We know that whosoever is born of God does not sin; but he that is begotten of God keeps himself, and that wicked one cannot touch him (see 1John 5:18).

Under the rules of engagement in job's day, God was looking for the best way to maximise wellness and long life for Job while satan was looking for the means of bringing about death. They were not in the same business.

> **God was not giving more grounds to satan, he was restricting him as best as he could under the limitations imposed by Adam's fall. If there was a way to impose more restrictions and still be just God would have done so. God tried his best.**

Why does satan incite God against Job?

Satan incited God because satan does not know ahead of time who will fall for his arguments. He has a scatter gun approach and hopes that someone would aid him in his dirty job and very often someone usually does. Satan prefers to hide rather than show himself to man as the direct cause of his misfortunes. He needed God to be his accomplice, but God would not.

> In whom the god of this world hath blinded the minds of them which believe not, lest the light of the glorious gospel of Christ, who is the image of God, should shine unto them.
> 2 Cor 4:4 (KJV)

Satan as the god of this world blinded the minds of the Sabeans, who hijacked and destroyed Job's business concerns and killed his servants who would have tried to stop the Sabeans.

> **God was not in control of those Sabeans. They were satan's hands and feet to bring destruction to Job.**

> Hast not thou made an hedge about him, and about his house, and about all that he hath on every side? thou hast blessed the work of his hands, and his substance is increased in the land.
>
> Job 1:10 (KJV)

Reading this episode in Job, one might come away with the idea that satan asks God permission before he attacks. Is this so? In the first instance, satan admits that there was a threefold hedge around Job. The weight of evidence from the scriptures implies that even Job was unaware of this hedge. The only reason why he would have been aware of this hedge would be because he had tried unsuccessfully to destroy Job, Job's house and his businesses. He figured that the hedge was the key hindrance.

The adversary had already attempted to wreck havoc in Job's life, his house and his possessions and that is how come he knew the boundaries of the hedge.

> **Satan had tested the hedge before he approached God. This means that satan does not ask God's permission before he attacks the people of God. He simply was looking for a way to talk God into withdrawing that hedge.**

Satan has always been the thief who steals, kills and destroys.

> Forasmuch then as the children are partakers of flesh and blood, he also himself likewise took part of the same; that through death he might destroy him that had the power of death, that is, the devil; And deliver them who through fear of death were all their lifetime subject to bondage.
>
> Hebrews 2:14-15 (KJV)

The question in the Old Testament was unanswered as to what gave Satan legal access to actually harm Job. This remained unanswered until the New Testament revealed the key to Satan's power to afflict. That key is the fear of death.

The conversation restated

In the light of what has been revealed to us in the New Testament, we can attempt an expanded version of that conversation between God and satan concerning Job.

I believe that the conversation really went like this:

> Satan approaches God and says "God, the fearful are subject to bondage all their lives.
> God responds with "Yes, that's true"
> Satan then says "I bring to your attention a three count charge against Job that Job is fearful of losing his health, his sons and daughters, and his possessions.
> Satan continues "You created Job with a will that gives him the capacity to make choices, right?"
> God responds "Yes, I am not a puppet master. I created a being capable of making choices. I want man to exercise his will and chose well."
> Satan continues "Well, can the same will not be used to choose that which is not good?"

Satan continues with a glint in his eyes "Job has asserted his will and by his own fear has given me opportunity to steal, kill and destroy. I really am going to exercise the right to bring his fears to pass. He is my captive"

With assurance in his voice he says sarcastically "This fellow Job has sown and he has to reap but try as I may, your mercy stops him from reaping the consequence to his fear. In my opinion you have violated his free will. God responds in mercy "do not put your hands on him."

Job had no redeemer. That was the best that God could do. I am convinced that what was called "The hedge" in Job's story is the very principle that David by revelation called the secret place of the most high!

Above all, taking the shield of faith, wherewith ye shall be able to quench all the fiery darts of the wicked.

Ephesians 6:16 (KJV)

Faith was revealed in a fuller measure in the New Testament, therefore the shield or hedge is strongest in the New Testament. It was fairly obvious during the earth walk of Jesus that various groups of men sought for ways to kill Jesus, the righteous one. You could say he was the only candle of light in a dark world. He stood out. They wanted him dead. Satan had taken note of him and also wanted him dead.

> And all in the synagogue were filled with a rage which boiled over in a sudden and angry outburst upon hearing these things, and having arisen, they threw Him outside of the city and led Him to an out jutting cliff of the mountain upon which their city stood built, so that they might hurl Him headlong down the precipice. But He himself, having passed through their midst, proceeded on His way.
>
> Luke 4:29-30 (Wuest)

Few can match the creativity of religious men as they yield their authority to co-create death with demonic spirits. Religious men have no qualms strategising the death of a fellow human being. In this story, Jesus is steered to the edge of the cliff by blood thirsty men who were planning to throw him down head first. In my mind's eye, I imagine

Jesus getting up and dusting himself had they carried that out. Perhaps knowing the uproar that would have ensued had he allowed them throw him headlong and then watched him dust himself and walk away, he chose the simpler of the solutions; he simply walks away from danger right through the midst of this mob.

Why could blood-thirsty men and satan not kill Jesus? Jesus was a master of using the shield of faith to quench all the fiery darts that satan sent his way. The shield of faith works by love. This shield of faith protected Jesus from the traps of wicked men and the prince of this world. Since his shield of faith was intact, it did not matter that the prince of this world came around. He could truly say that, "the prince of this world cometh and hath nothing in me," (See John 14:30).

When your faith shield is functional it does not really matter what strategies are being hatched against you nor does it matter what the nor does it matter what the adversary is up to. The shield of faith will quench every single fiery dart of the wicked one.

This shield of faith was intact in the life of Jesus until Jesus exercised his will to die. At that time the hedge began to shrink. That hedge shrunk so much until he could be arrested at the garden of Gethsemane.

How did the hedge surrounding Jesus get dismantled? God did not dismantle it. Satan did not dismantle it. Jesus did.

> Thinkest thou that I cannot now pray to my
> Father, and he shall presently give me more
> than twelve legions of angels?
> Matthew 26:53 (KJV)

A roman legion consists of 6000 soldiers. We know from the Old Testament that one angel took out 185,000 men in one night. When Jesus said that the Father would give him twelve legions, he meant that at that very instance, should Jesus request it, God would have released 72,000 angels to come to his rescue.. Those angels would have done everything possible to minister deliverance to Jesus. That atmosphere of betrayal coupled with the blood thirsty mob was not dangerous for Jesus, it was the safest place to be because the hedge of protection was still in place. Jesus was protected and he knew it.

Jesus had angelic help at his beck and call. He admitted that he had it, but by an exercise of his will, he chose not to ask for supernatural deliverance from God. Once he had exercised his will in this way, he was applying the blows that broke down the hedge of protection. It is a fact worth noting that the more the will of man is strongly exercised, the harder it is for God's mercy to overrule.

> 17 Therefore doth my Father love me,
> because I lay down my life, that I might take
> it again.
> 18 No man taketh it from me, but I lay
> it down of myself. I have power to lay it
> down, and I have power to take it again.
> This commandment have I received of my
> Father.
> John 10:17-18 (KJV)

The power of death is in the tongue of man

Jesus, as a man, had the power to lay down and take up his life again if he chose to. He, in his perfect humanity, chose to lay it down. His life was not taken from him. He laid it down willingly.

He used the words of his mouth to remove the shield of faith. Somewhere between Gethsemane and the cross, Jesus set his will in a I-am-ready-to-die mode. Only then could he die.

The hedge around Job is very much like the shield of faith which quenches all the fiery darts of the wicked one. In effect the hedge around Job was Job cooperating with the protection of God's mercy by using the shield of faith. If Job stops cooperating with God, through fear, what can God do? Even then, God does not fly away like one who is easily hurt. God still extends his mercy to protect.

> **However, due to the exercise of man's will, in fear and unbelief, the extent of that hedge is shrunken by man. As the boundary of the hedge shrinks, satan's surface of attack widens.**

Does the New Testament not portray God as one who sends delusions to men?

> 10 And with all deceivableness of unrighteousness in them that perish; because they received not the love of the truth, that they might be saved.
> 11 And for this cause God shall send them strong delusion, that they should believe a lie:
> 12 That they all might be damned who believed not the truth, but had pleasure in

unrighteousness.

2 Thessalonians 2:10-12 (KJV)

The people under discussion are people that perish because they did not receive the love of truth. Normally people would submit to anything if they are intimidated for a sustained period. There are people that don't really love God that just want to avoid an unfavorable situation. God does not harass people into submission. When people reject the truth, with each rejection, they become more hardened.. They become what the bible refers to as hard hearted.

Why would God send a strong delusion?

This strong delusion is not just some random happening to strike fear into the heart of the believer. These people who have been sent a strong delusion are people who already qualified themselves as not loving the truth. God who is absolute righteousness and Justice is also immutable, so we know he cannot lie. He, who is truth did not create any human being not to love the truth. These men made their choice when they did not receive the love of the truth. We know that God is not interested in the death of a sinner, but in their repentance, (2 Peter 3:9), therefore, he will do his best to give them opportunity after opportunity to accept the salvation of God willingly.

You ask yourself, "When a person does not love the truth, what does he love?"He loves and believes the lie.

This is a reference to people who prefer deception. They are deluded and they love it. Sometimes these people need an emphatic means by which the slant of their own heart is made plain to them so they can set their heart on a choice.

What is meant by God sending them strong delusion? It means that when people are stoutly against the truth, God has to respect their will ultimately. He cannot be just if after they continue to reject the Lord and his truth he prevents them from reaping the harvest of hating the truth.

God creates opportunities for them to back out on their stance, but they resolutely chose delusion in a way that is binding. They close the door of repentance on themselves. This alters the course of their lives. They are on a slippery slope brought about by the strength of their choices.

6

Who is this Judge?

2 Saying, There was in a city a judge, which feared not God, neither regarded man:

3 And there was a widow in that city; and she came unto him, saying, Avenge me of mine adversary.

4 And he would not for a while: but afterward he said within himself, Though I fear not God, nor regard man;

5 Yet because this widow troubleth me, I will avenge her, lest by her continual coming she weary me.6 And the Lord said, Hear what the unjust judge saith.

Luke 18:2-6 (KJV)

Kenneth Wuest renders the third verse as "Now, there was a widow in that city, and she kept on coming to him at recurring intervals, saying, Protect me by an equitable administration of justice from my opponent in a lawsuit." This woman came asking to be avenged of her enemies. She actually kept on coming at recurring intervals in her words.

The judge is aloof and does not plan to avenge her. The manner of her coming through words troubled the judge. We know that the way to trouble this judge is to come through words.

> **The continual affirmation of the word of God ultimately wearies this judge. In effect, words fitly framed and sent on assignment will dismantle the apparent indifference of the judge towards the initial petition.**

We know that this judge lingered for a while before budging. Could it be because he wanted to be bribed by the widow before he decides in her favour? This reminds me of the Governor Felix of Caesarea that used to call for the Apostle Paul to appear frequently before him in order that he might receive some bribe from Paul (See Acts 24:26).

> Lest by her continual coming she weary me.
> Luke 18:5c (KJV)

The thought of her continual coming sets the judge thinking. He then gives in.

Students of the Greek New Testament tell us that there is a play on words here that is lost on the English reader. We are told that the Greek phrase means to "strike under the eye" or to give a black eye.

This does not mean that the widow gave the judge a blow to the face. It is symbolic language, a figure of speech, and not to be taken literally. Just as a black eye is on the face and unpleasant to behold, the expression means that the reputation is damaged. He needs a PR exercise. The unjust judge was motivated by keeping appearances. He needed to be seen as a good guy but all the while he is open to be bribed.

> **Even though this judge has no regard for the woman's welfare, he is deeply sensitive to himself. This judge will ultimately judge even though his judgments are not a product of a love for man or some principle of piety.**

What did this unjust judge say?

By this judge's admission, we gather that he can be troubled. When he is troubled he will change his mind and pass judgment. We know the secret that he can be wearied.

Take note that the Lord Jesus, that is the gospel himself, called this judge unjust. Something about this judge does not quite sit right. When someone is described as unjust, that does not convey a good feel does it? The big point that the Lord is getting across is in the words that he puts in the mouth of the unjust judge in this parable. Jesus said we should hear what the unjust judge says.

> "though I neither fear God nor regard man,
>
> yet... I will avenge her." (See Luke 18:4-5)

The only person that this judge does not have issues with is the adversary! This judge does not fear God. He does not care about the widow.

The unmistakable idea is that since the judge did not fear God he should not have vindicated the widow. This enigmatic judge grudgingly agreed to vindicate her for other reasons.

We know instinctively that vindicating this widow is the right thing to do, but this judge hesitated. Therefore the two qualities that hinder the vindication are negative. The dominant characteristics of this judge are the very obstacles to his taking sides with the widow against the adversary. In the first instance, the real reason why he was unable to readily help this woman was because he had no fear of God.

This is proof positive that the fear of God would have caused that judge to judge in favour of that widow. If we were in that judge's shoes, the fear of God within us would cause us to help that needy widow. Wouldn't it? That being the case, God who embodies the fear of the Lord, would definitely show mercy to that widow.

This parable addresses our prejudices against God. If a judge, an unjust one for that matter, who confesses his lack of godly fear, admits that he can find a reason to bend his twisted methods in order to vindicate this widow, we can be infinitely certain that God, who is just, and who uses his strength to daily load us with benefits, will help his own.

It starts getting clearer that in true Lucan style he is telling us that God is not like the unjust judge.

God will vindicate you.

The more you read that parable, the more the curiosity is raised as to the enigmatic judge and his mysterious ways. The identity of this judge is important. Who is this judge that would relate to a widow this way?

> 6 And the Lord said, Hear what the unjust
> judge saith.
> Luke 18:6 (KJV)

Jesus said to hear what the unjust judge said. Spiritual beings are not necessarily known by what they look like. Outward appearances can be deceptive. By God's design, ours is a universe governed by words. You can tell a lot about a person by what he says. Some people think that if a being looks like God, then it must be God. That type of reasoning can get you in trouble. You know God by what he says. The same goes for other spirit beings. In the words of the unjust judge, we find the secrets of his attributes, his methods as well as the proper rules of engagement. He shows us how to enforce the desired outcome.

What the judge says, he says within himself. They were not a conversation with the widow. The widow would have noticed the hesitation on the part of the judge, but would not have been privy to his reasoning.

There are some that assume that this unjust judge refers to God since this is a parable about prayer. Does this add up scripturally? This judge did not fear God. He did not base his judgments on religious grounds. We are told that this judge did not care for man, he can be wearied, and his mind can be changed. Is this God? Consider the following:

> What is man that thou art mindful of him,
> and the son of man that thou visitest him?
> Psalm 8:4 (KJV)

What is man that thou shouldst magnify him, and that thou shouldst set thine heart upon him?

Job 7:17 (KJV)

Lord, what is man that thou takest knowledge of him, or the son of man that thou makest account of him

Psalm 144:3 (KJV)

The question "What is man?" is repeatedly asked in scripture. Man looks around him perplexed as to why God has chosen to give man a central place in his plan. That's because we look at the wrong man. The man that God reckons with is Jesus. In the light of what Jesus is, everything about man makes sense.

That God sets his own heart upon man, takes knowledge of man, magnifies him and is mindful of man is clearly documented in scripture. God says concerning himself, "I am the Lord I change not." It is said of God that there is no variableness about him or shadow of turning. God is a just God. The reason why the unjust judge gave in to the widow is because he was shielding himself from getting wearied by the widow. The unjust judge is really self-serving; he did not care about the widow. He answered the widow out of selfish irritation. The love nature of God is not obvious in this unjust judge. This is significant. This is a big give-away that helps us understand in plain terms that we are not to confuse this unjust judge for God.

Whoever this judge is, we can be sure of this, he cannot be the God of the New Creation, the Father of glory.

> **In stark contrast to the depiction of this unjust judge, we can expect much better treatment from God than the widow ever received from that cold callous godless loveless judge. God's dealings with us are defined by his everlasting love.**

Knowing Luke's style, we see that the point was made in the contrast. The thinking is that if the unjust judge will answer will answer the widow that he did not love or care about, how much more will the God who loves us release answers to us when we pray?

To press the point further, from this parable, we do not approach our loving Father the way that the woman approached the unjust judge. When you think of the unjust judge, just declare to yourself, "this is not the picture of my heavenly Father who gave himself for me at great cost." The parable is a powerful contrast and not a description of God's modus operandi. God does not reason or operate like that unjust judge.

Now that we know that God does not qualify as the unjust judge, we must investigate further. The qualities of the unjust judge does not also represent the ministry of angels. The angels of God hearken to the voice of God's word and they minister for the heirs of salvation.

> **The qualities of this unjust judge most definitely resemble those of the spirit being that the bible refers to as satan.**

Could this unjust judge be the devil? Satan is naturally a strong candidate if not for the fact that we are told that the widow approached the judge because she had an adversary. The widow wanted to be avenged of her adversary. The judge was going to deliver the sentence in favour of the widow against the adversary.

The devil is clearly in the camp of the adversary. The devil therefore is not the judge. Who then is this unjust judge?

> And you, that were sometime alienated and
> enemies in your mind by wicked
> works, yet now hath he reconciled.
> Colossians 1:21 (KJV)

Why is it that Christians experience spectacularly beneath the provisions of God? The new birth is a new creation of the spirit. Yet, even though we are new spirits, we experience far beneath the purpose and plan of God. The reason is that according to the revelation that God gave to Paul, the enmity and alienation between man and God is in man's mind.

> **The mind of man stoutly seized the rulership over man and led man into a delusional state, spiritually speaking. The mind is the center of alienation from God.**

A born again man whose mind is not renewed to the word of God will continue to experience alienation from God because the mind, which is responsible for alienation is also responsible for transformation.

> 5-8 The carnal attitude sees no further than natural things. But the spiritual attitude reaches out after the things of the spirit. The former attitude means, bluntly, death: the latter means life and inward peace. And this is only to be expected, for the carnal attitude is inevitably opposed to the purpose of God, and neither can nor will follow his laws for living. Men who hold this attitude cannot possibly please God.
> Romans 8:5-8 (JB Phillips)

The mind of man holds man in the land of captivity. To say it the way JB Phillips so beautifully expressed it in his translation "The former attitude means, bluntly, death."

> **The mind will comfortably co-create death with the adversary.**
> **Inward peace is experienced as we allow our mind co-create**
> **peace with the word of God.**

And be not conformed to this world: but be ye transformed by the renewing of your mind, that ye may prove what is that good, and acceptable, and perfect, will of God.
Romans 12:2 (KJV)

And stop assuming an outward expression that does not come from within you and is not representative of what you are in your inner being but is patterned after this age; but change your outward expression to one that comes from within and is representative of your inner being, by the renewing of your mind, resulting in your putting to the test what is the will of God, the good and well-pleasing and complete will, and having found that it meets specifications, place your approval upon it.

Romans 12:2 (Wuest)

There are genuine Christians who present their bodies as a living sacrifice to God but function largely from a mind that is not renewed to the word of God. Through the avenue of the unrenewed mind they still experience feelings of alienation, fear, depression and all manner of captivity, these are the very same patterns that the world lives by. The unrenewed mind stops them from proving God's will. The word of God tells us that our transformation does not depend on God, the devil or the world.

Why are we told to renew our minds?

It is so that we can prove the will of God. You can only prove that which exists. This means that no matter what God's will for our lives are, we can be hindered from enjoying the grandeur of them by retaining an unrenewed mind.

There is a component in the soul of man that listens, computes, analyses and compares in order to arrive at a verdict. Since we are transformed by the renewing of our minds, it would mean that anything that will successfully hinder the believer from transformation will have to operate via the mind of man. We use the legal document of God's word to train our minds, and this is what it means to approach the unjust judge.

That the unjust judge manifests characteristics more akin to that of the devil is without dispute. The carnal mind is not subject to the law of God. Through the fall of Adam the carnal mind has learned the ways and methods of a fallen angel. This leaves us with only one other candidate in the word of God that is referred to as the enemy of God. The carnal mind is enmity against God.

> **The unrenewed mind is the unjust judge and is the door that the adversary uses to hinder the manifestation of God's purpose and plan.**

On a purely experiential level, it is mind boggling the volume of negative things that you believe to be true about yourself, God and the devil on a daily basis!

Our minds are forever entertaining ideas, reasoning and philosophies that are framed to do us damage. If you leave the unjust judge to listen to the adversary's arguments alone, your emotions will closely mirror those of the world around you. In practical terms, the adversary does not play fair in the courtroom of your mind. When you find your thoughts overwhelmed by the lies of satan, you are to raise your voice above the noise playing in your emotional life by voicing God's word. The unjust judge represents a problem that all believers face, namely that we are willing to listen to lies about who we are until we really believe the lie and forget who we really are. Consider the operation of the unjust judge in proverbs.

> The lazy man says in his heart that there is a
> lion in the street.
> Proverbs 26:13(KJV)

This is not a wise man. All the wise men understand the implied wisdom of diligence. This fellow who says that there is a lion in the street has a strong excuse.

This is the excuse that his adversary has injected into his imagination. This prevents him from taking his place in life. He reasons that this world is a wicked world, and decides to stay indoors. The word assures him that the lion of Judah is on his side. This does not register on his imagination. He is unwilling to go to war against the thought that there is a lion in the street.

It is a lazy mind that fabricates a lion that locks him in a prison. There are others that were sold the same lie who chose to go out about their daily chores nonetheless. He thinks that the presence of the troops determines the outcomes. He is convinced that the walls have to disappear before he can move. He does not know that by his God he scales over imposing walls. He is unaware that by the energizing of God he runs through troops.

That which is arrayed against you does not need to disappear.
By your words you are scaling over and overrunning the tricks of the wicked one.

Consider two Christians in marriage union. The unwise wife has spoken sharply to her husband. The furious husband has decided that his manliness has been challenged. He wants to settle the whole fiasco with blows. He believes that some women do not respond to the word of God but to blows. The unwise wife uses the sharp tongue until the husband batters her into subjugation with upper cuts, kicks and slaps.

He repeats this often enough while cooperating with his wife's sharp tongue. His marriage is a hell. His mind has fainted from acting on the word. He is praying earnestly, but his stout words set him on a collision with the word. Soon he gives up praying. He thinks prayer has failed. He has fainted. His first conclusion is that it is the devil's fault. This brother should first appeal to the unjust judge of his unrenewed mind.

That judge is delivering the judgment on the supremacy of blows. His appeal is the confession that agrees with God about what to do in those situations. This causes him to live out a new way of thinking and living. This makes him unmanageable by the adversary. Here is a 40 year old Christian chap who feels a sharp pain on the chest. His lightning fast mind recalls that his uncle and Dad both died of hypertension when they turned 39. His mind assures him that the sharp pain is hypertension. His mind gets all religious on him and assures him that at 40 years, he has already outlived both his father and his uncle. That he has already tried and heaven understands. That he is a son that the celestial city wants home. These are arguments assaulting his mind.

He is getting conditioned for death. His mind supplies reasons backed with facts, dates and emotions why it is time to die. Our experiences have had unfettered access to our minds from birth. Through this access we have become conditioned.

> **The unjust judge operates on the fallen mind of Adam. The adversary says things that are contrary to us in the court of life. Except we hold fast to the confession of that hope that we find in God's word, we find that we are siding in with the adversary in our words!**

If you are hoping to manifest the emotion of joy but find yourself tempted by melancholy, you do not have to give in to the adversary of sorrow. If you don't have the emotions that you need, you use your words to assault the reasoning of the judge until a decision for healthy emotions is reached. Your words are calling for an alternate set of emotions to sadness. You weary your judge out of sadness.

> **Become as actively intolerant of the unrenewed mind as you are the devil!**

7

Delays

"….And he kept on being unwilling to do so
for a considerable time."

Luke 18:4a (Wuest)

The phrase "for a while" shows the passage of time. Supposing that the unjust judge is a reference to God, many people grow weary because it is inevitable that their delays are due to some mysterious plan in God. They have been neutralised by buying into the reasoning of the adversary. We faint in prayer because we believe the wrong things about God. In turn the wrong thinking and believing cause us to draw back from responding to God by faith.

We now know that the unrenewed mind is the unjust judge. It is not that God finds it easier to answer some requests faster than he does others. God is not the variable. The readiness of the human mind to agree with God is the great variable.

You are well aware that your mind is not equally persuaded about all issues of life. Wherever your mind is persuaded to agree with God's word, you free yourself to experience the manifestation of God's plan faster. Using the language of the book of Romans, you reduce the time it takes you to prove the will of God. There are other areas where your mind is more alienated from the word of God. In these areas it needs a lot more renewing. This extends the proving time.

> **Does God find some prayers easier to answer than others? It is not that God finds some issues relatively easier to revolve than others. God is not the variable. The readiness of the human mind to cooperate with God is the great variable in enjoying answered prayers.**

> 7 And shall not God avenge his own elect, which cry day and night unto him, though he bear long with them?
> 8 I tell you that he will avenge them speedily. Nevertheless when the Son of man cometh, shall he find faith on the earth?
> Luke 18:7-8 (KJV)

Jesus plainly teaches that God avenges his own elect speedily. This means that God supplies answers to prayer speedily. It is important that we are able to identify who this personality is that is referred to as the *"He that bears long with them."* Unmasking this *"He that bears long"* is not a trivial exercise.

I understand why some would conclude that the "He that bears long" is descriptive of God. Long ago I used to think and approach things from this mindset too. Let us remind ourselves that all through this verse Luke is illustrating things about God and how God avenges. Seen that way, I interpreted this to mean that God was the subject matter all through; therefore God will avenge the elect though he takes long to do it.

The trouble was that I knew that in the same parable Jesus had actually said that God avenges his own elect speedily! How could I reconcile this with my belief that he also bears long? We have clear statement that it is the unjust judge that "would not for a while" (See Luke 18:4). We are correct to say that the unjust judge bears long. He waits for as long as he possibly can before judging in our favour. This leads us to say that the judge that "would not for a while" is the same as "he that bears long". God avenges speedily but there is another that delays as long as he can.

Luke is contrasting God's characteristics with that of another. Luke is contrasting God's willingness with the dithering, wavering and unwilling stance of this unjust judge. The unjust judge is really held up as a showcase of that which is unlike God. The disciple should not approach God anticipating that God will hold out from giving an answer as long as he can delay. That forces us to treat God as we would the unjust judge. Jesus is dismantling religious strongholds that present God as one who is hard to be entreated, a God who delays just because he can and sometimes because of mysterious reasons not revealed to man. The Bible presents the unselfishness of God.

> **The person that is taking a while to answer is not God. If you do not know this, you will be hopelessly confused about prayer not knowing whether God will be favorable or not. You must realize that God does not say "No" where his word already says, "Yes." He never says no to his own word.**

God calls those making a request to him, his elects. He admits that there is some relationship. They are his and he is theirs. In the parable, the judge of that city is unrelated to that woman. That judge maintains a cold aloofness on his lofty throne.

Some will ask, "If God answers speedily, why then do we see a delay?" When you pray, you are talking to a God that hears and answers speedily. When it comes to manifestation of the answer, others get involved. There is a God-side and a man-side to receiving manifestation to prayer. The manifestation of our desire involves a process of bearing long. Involved in this process is the unjust judge. God is responsible for answering speedily but the unjust judge is involved in bringing forth the manifestation of those answers that God has given you.

> **Your prayer appeals to God. Your prayer also appeals to your mind. While God answers speedily, if your mind is unrenewed you are unable to make the adjustments that receives the answers. Until our mind has come to a place of conviction, we don't act like we have the answer even though God has released it. This causes delay to manifestation.**

Deferred hope piles pressure on our heart to give up. This means that when there is delay and we do not refresh our image with the word, we faint. The unjust judge delays; he takes a while to arrive at a judgment and is willing to admit all available arguments before deciding.

The dominant characteristic of the unjust judge that Jesus is dwelling on is that of delay. He zeroes in on the fact that God speedily supplies answers to his elect.

When some people notice delays, their first conclusion is that God is responsible for the delay and is using it to teach some mysterious lesson or the other. These hold God responsible for delays when they should suspect the activities of the unjust judge and the actions of the adversary.

I tell you that he will avenge them speedily.

Nevertheless when the Son of man cometh,

shall he find faith on the earth?

Luke 18:8 (KJV)

The Son of man looks for faith on the earth. He his hindered by unbelief while his purposes are advanced by faith. Delay is not due to heavenly wrath but to earthly limitations.

The greatest limitation is imposed by unbelief. This means that we can hinder God's speedy response by not operating in faith. This is a man-made delay.

Delays do occur, but when there are delays we don't need to bombard heaven to release to us the very things that God already says belong to us, we simply strip our minds of unbelief and press on in faith. You see, the widow according to this parable does not wait on God for the manifestation for God is not the cause of her delay. She, together with all people of faith waits with God.

8

Seeing Clearly

And it is this message which we have heard from Him and at present is ringing in our ears and we are bringing back tidings to you, that God as to His nature is light, and darkness in Him does not exist, not even one particle.

1 John 1:5 (Wuest)

All of us! Nothing between us and God, our faces shining with the brightness of his face. And so we are transfigured much like the Messiah, our lives gradually becoming brighter and more beautiful as God enters our lives and we become like him.

2 Cor. 3:18 (The Message)

The message that we hear about God is deeply important. Many people take these things as theological positions and points of doctrine to argue about, but it is a matter of life and death. It is not enough that God is light with no iota of darkness, if that is not what we have heard about him.

You are limited to what you have heard about God. Why is it important that we develop an accurate image of God? It is so that our minds have a clear picture to transform us to. I cannot be gentler than my God, that is impossible. It is also true that I cannot be more kind than my thoughts concerning him. If what I hear about him is that he is sometimes light and at other times darkness, it is understandable when my character reflects my belief and I manifest instability.

It is God's intention that we have a clear picture of his true nature because that is also the explanation of ours.

It matters that we see the truth constantly in the face of God. Whatever I picture God to be in nature and character is really a prophecy of my future.

> **People who believe in a mysterious God ultimately become unstable and unpredictable in their daily lives even if in reality God is not mysterious. The reason for this is that we are transformed by what we see and believe.**

You can appreciate why the greatest strategy of the adversary is to corrupt our minds concerning God. This is interesting because though many believers will readily admit that satan wages war, they fail to realise that the war is not waged in the skies but in the minds of men!

It is a battle of belief. In this war, there is no force involved, but deceptive reasoning aimed at seducing the mind away from the truth of God especially concerning his nature and character. The adversary skilfully misrepresents God to man. Since he has done this over thousands of years, he gains tremendous cumulative authority from deceiving man to believe falsehoods about God. One man's lie becomes the belief system of a whole community with time depending on how influential the man is.

When man is deceived, that deception stops him from seeing God as He is and from cooperating with the God of the Bible. The man with the unrenewed mind is hoodwinked into cooperating with the product of his own reasoning. Except I know the truth, deception creates a false image of God for me.

> **The man with an unrenewed mind often assumes that he is grappling with the God of the bible, but he is really projecting his own thoughts and worshipping his projections in the name of religion. This is why religion is deadly.**

Religious people are responsible for a lot of massacres in history. This is understandable in the light of what the word of God really says. People who are gullible fall prey to satan's tricks and the desires of their own flesh. They blame their cravings on God and find some remote verses of scripture taken out of context to support it, and much death follows. They think that that have killed, maimed and wasted lives in the name of the Lord, but they have shown their (mis)understanding of God. What they have done is consistent with their unrenewed mind and completely out of sync with God.

When men say that they doubt God's goodness, they say that because they have not seen him. What they doubt unconsciously is their cumulative ideas about God.

> **Truth is a big deal. It matters what we have heard about God. It matters what we believe to be true about God. This is because we grow into whatever we accept as true concerning God.**

If your truth is not God's truth, you will reap the harvest of your belief systems. For the spiritual principle holds true, "be it unto you according to your faith."

That spiritual principle means that you will ultimately become in character what you believe God is like. It is as we see him with an open face that we build into our daily walk the same substance and quality of perfection that we see in him.

We cannot be transformed beyond the extent to which our minds are renewed to the reality of God in his word. This means that our transformation into what God is has a boundary. That boundary is how much of the true picture of his person and face that we allow ourselves to see in the person of Jesus.

> **If I believe that God is harsh, I will become harsh. If I believe that God is controlling, I will exhibit more of the same even if God is not that way. It is important we understand these principles of our human constitution. We feed on our belief systems.**

6 But let him ask in faith, nothing wavering. For he that wavereth is like a wave of the sea driven with the wind and tossed.

7 For let not that man think that he shall receive any thing of the Lord.

8 A double minded man is unstable in all his ways.

James 1:6-8 (KJV)

If I think that God is unpredictable, I waver when I approach him. I think I am that way because I am being like God, but James says I am being like the waves of the sea! I have a double mind about God because I believe what I think about him rather than what he says in his own word. I then become unstable in my own ways though God is forever stable in his. I am then boxed into a corner where I cannot receive anything of him. I think he is not giving whereas I am the one not receiving. This is my way, not God's way. If God is light, and my projection of him is that he is also darkness, then in order to develop fully into him I will manifest both light and darkness. This is inescapable.

In the final analysis you become whatever your mind thinks your God is like. You cannot ultimately live any purer than your comprehension of God.

The darkness that we sometimes attribute to God is largely a reflection of how dark our thought life had descended.

O taste and see that the Lord is good: blessed
is the man that trusteth in him.
Psalm 34.8 (KJV)

There is a blessedness, a supernatural empowering that flows from an understanding of God's goodness. We are only able to enjoy that blessedness as we trust in him instead of trusting in our thoughts concerning him. Experience often pushes people to say that God is not good. They are tasting their experiences instead of tasting God.

God is good whether we know it or not. It is our taste buds that free us to see his goodness. Poor spiritual food leads to spiritual blindness. Spiritual blindness is simply a lack of understanding of how good God is.

You are what you eat. If in your comprehension you are dealing with a sometimes good and sometimes not-so-good God, that is exactly what you will taste when you feast on him. You then see more proof in your experience that validates your mistrust of the goodness of God. In our Christian walk, we taste what we think of him, but it is the intention of God that you develop good spiritual taste buds that allow you to throw away junk and feast on the rich cuisine served out directly from the goodness of God himself. Don't eat imitation spiritual food, go for the original in the word and let that food change you forever.

9

Standing on the Word

Therefore every scribe which is instructed unto the kingdom of heaven is like unto a man that is an householder, which bringeth forth out of his treasure things new and old. Matthew 13:52 (KJV)

Every man learned in the sacred scriptures who has accepted the precepts and instructions with reference to the kingdom of heaven is like a man who is a master of a house, who is of such a character that he dispenses with hearty enjoyment out of his treasure-house, things new as to quality and also things mellowed with age by reason of use. Matthew 13:52 (Wuest)

Jesus recommends that we should be instructed unto the kingdom of heaven. Christians need instruction. He places premium on understanding the word. It is the understanding of God's word that makes you a householder spiritually speaking. You are unable to possess that which you do not understand even if it is yours. A householder is a believer who has gained mastery over his house. This house is the structure that the word has built in your life through understanding. That structure is the human heart. Treat your heart as you would treat a bank vault, for the heart is the treasure house.

God has placed within your reborn spirit tremendous wealth. It is as you get understanding through the word that you begin to gain access into what is yours. That access allows you to bring out of the deposit of God within you.

"No word" simply means "no access". There are supernatural machinery that you can pull out of your heart because God has placed them within you. These are spiritual machines that you use to build out all that you need in your world. You gain mastery in the use of these spiritual machinery through the understanding of the word. Jesus gave this teaching after delivering the powerful teaching on the operation of God's word as a seed. This means that just like an acorn carries within it information about how to produce the mighty oak tree, the word carries the image within itself of the end result.

This parable of Jesus about the seed operation of God's word is the most important parable in the whole of God's word. Any smart farmer knows the importance of seeds. You and God farm together as co-labourers. He wants you to give uttermost attention to the seed of his word. You must learn to give God's word first place in your life.

> 14 The sower soweth the word.
>
> 15 And these are they by the way side, where
>
> the word is sown; but when they have heard,
>
> Satan cometh immediately, and taketh away
>
> the word that was sown in their hearts.
>
> Mark 4:14-15 (KJV)

There are many things to be said about this parable. We know that God has entrusted man with sowing seed. The Bible declares that we overcome by the word of our testimony. The testimony is not the secret ingredient, the word of God within the testimony. The seed that many people sow is their testimony and their experiences. That is not what the Lord Jesus recommended. Experiences and testimonies have their place but only as far as the word contained within that testimony. Do not base your life on testimonies, but on the word. The seed we are to sow is God's word.

It is a most interesting fact that in this parable, Jesus does not even say anything about those who have not heard the word. It is as though, until one hears the word, he is not spiritually relevant. All the categories of people that Jesus comments on in this parable have something in common, they all heard the word. Even though not all of them brought forth the desired harvest, they at least took the first step of giving place to God's word. Our heart is the bag that we use to hold the seed of God's word. We then use our mouth to spread that word into our environment.

Jesus teaches that when the people in this parable have heard the word, satan cometh immediately. In this case, satan did not come because anyone went out of their way to invite him by acting like the black sheep of the family of man. He came because the person involved had done a dangerous thing – they had heard the word. This is an instance where satan brings trouble because someone has done the right thing.

When you do good by hearing the word, the initial response is not necessarily favourable, but rest in the fact that the word that you are hearing will frame your world to align with the intention and will of God.

The word of God is his mechanism for transferring his thoughts into your world so that these thoughts become your experience. It contains within it the image of goodness and it will ultimately birth into your world a lasting tasteful goodness that nothing can shake. The beginning does not necessarily look rosy, but anyone who is a word practitioner, understands that the word causes us to finish powerfully.

The word of God is spiritual seed and, like all seeds, it must be planted in order for it to release the life contained within it.

The word that is not planted is like seed kept within an airtight jar. It retains its power but none of it is released to bring about change.

The word of God is not likened to magic, it is likened to seed. The magical effect of God's word is more myth than reality. Don't treat the word like an amulet. Years ago when I used to have nightmares, I placed the Bible under my pillow supposing that by some magical means the word inside the Bible will ward off the demonic spirits. The nightmares became more rampant! Treating the word more like some mystical item, people carry the Bible everywhere they go. It is in their pockets. It is in their wardrobe. It is in their living room gathering dust over the mantelpiece.

Though the word of God is seed, you don't plant it by letting dust settle over it at home or anywhere for that matter. If that's the way it works, we should all buy truckloads of Bibles and plant them all over our garden. The word is not magic, it is spiritual seed that meets any need. It must be planted in order to realise its potential.

What is implied by "they heard the word?"

There is nothing to hear if nothing has been spoken. Hearing implies that sounds have been released. In this parable, Jesus is likening a preacher's preaching of the word to a farmer scattering seed. This means that when sound is given to God's word, the kingdom of God is set in motion by the speaker and the hearer. The speaker and the hearer are often different but it is more impactful when the speaker is also the hearer.

> **The word of God is seed. You plant it in order to release its life. You plant it into your human heart by saying and hearing it.**

From this parable, it would appear that satan is more aware of the power of the word as seed than the average human is. He is more prone to move immediately the word is heard. He does this while the hearer is still somewhat unconvinced.

> **Satan is mostly able to steal the word immediately if we lack understanding of what we have heard.**

How brilliant it will be when the believer starts responding to the word promptly. What a shock it will be to religious spirits! We also see that when people start hearing the word of God, satan is unsettled in a major way. The word carries within it the power to bring the image of heaven into the earth. If the word is allowed to work, there is no end to the victories that can be reaped through diligence.

The planted word does not only cause a stir on the inside of the hearer, it causes panic within the enemy too. The enemy knows that he is no match for the word. In order to stop the working of the word, he attempts to distract the Christian. He sends some trouble. In this scenario, this trouble is not because the Christian is reaping the wrong seeds he has sown, but because he is doing the right thing and has to be stopped by all means at the enemy's disposal. The enemy is after the word. The devil could care less if you drive a Bentley or a Maybach. He only goes after the Bentley in order to unsettle the confidence that the believer has in the word.

Too many people buy into the myth that the presence of trouble is proof positive that the one experiencing the trouble is godless and wicked. Jesus, while delivering the granddaddy of all parables tells us that satan can come because you are hearing the word.

Hearing the word is the genesis of all supernatural living. It is the right thing to do. Jesus teaches us that there are afflictions and persecutions that arise for the word's sake. Consider what Peter says along these same lines concerning the trouble that can be suffered for doing the right things in a fallen world.

Acting on the word in the workplace

18 Servants, be subject to your masters with all fear; not only to the good and gentle, but also to the forward.

19 For this is thankworthy, if a man for conscience toward God endure grief, suffering wrongfully.

20 For what glory is it, if, when ye be buffeted for your faults, ye shall take it patiently? but if, when ye do well, and suffer for it, ye take it patiently, this is acceptable with God.

1 Peter 2:18-20 (KJV)

There are bad managers and there are good ones. I guess you already know that. Peter is coming down to the basics. Given that we are called to show forth the praises of God in a fallen world, what does Christianity look like in a hostile world like that which exists in the workplace?

> **You know that you are the righteousness of God in Christ Jesus.**

The grief spoken of in the 19th verse is a word that implies mental anguish and grief, and so is not physical. When he says conscience towards God, he means that the reason why the man does this is because he is God-conscious. Only a person who is God-conscious can receive and live out the instruction from Peter.

As we stay God-conscious, there is a grace supplied from that consciousness that causes us to live supernaturally. Without that God–consciousness, the average Joe will read this, shake his head and conclude that living this way is beyond his grasp.

> **The consciousness of God affects you to the point where you take that divine consciousness more seriously than any injustice suffered when offenses are committed against you.**

The flesh is well developed in bitterness and retaliation and for the man of the flesh the answer is pretty obvious. The answer for the man of the spirit shocks the senses. Peter is overthrowing the usual way of doing things. What Peter is discussing is not valid for the unbeliever because

He does not admit the Lordship of the word and Jesus is not his Lord

A Christian understands the lordship of the word. We understand and expect that the unbeliever under similar conditions would bring out armoured tanks and weapons of war when treated unfairly for doing the right thing. That is not the believer's walk. Peter is not adding a new idea to our well-established thought patterns, he is asking for a revolution of thought because we are those made alive with Christ from the dead.

> **We are often so focused on the actions of those who are not treating us nicely that we fail to realise that the major challenge we face is a failure to understand that our flesh also does not treat us right.**

The flesh does not generate godly thoughts. The righteousness of God in Christ will rise up above the noise of the flesh by choosing the word over the world.

Too many times we allow the flesh to crowd us into panic. This causes us to take matters into our own hands. The grace of God causes us to rise above panic because we are righteous. Righteousness enables us not to act ugly even when others are.

The flesh convinces us that the bad treatment from the manager is between us and the manager. The flesh deceives us to pay him back in his own coin. We will pay the manager from hell back in his own coin. Righteous people that we are, we know that the whole scenario is between us, the manager and God. The evil manager ignores God and acts ugly while we base our response on the indwelling life of God within us. That day is not far when we will hear properly word-adjusted people say, "It is true, I have been treated really badly and dealt an ugly hand; and yes, these wicked managers deserve to reap what they have sown; but no, I am blood-bought and because of the blood of Jesus I will not slander; I am blessed so I will bless rather than curse."

Flipping the coin on its head, a Christian, who is a manager, reading this understands that we should manage people by the word of God. Something of a divine invasion will happen in the work place when word-minded people start managing people by the word in the office. The office is the way it is because few Christian managers plant the word at work. I am not referring to some evangelism drive, but to Christians, managers, who have gone to business school, now sitting in front of the word learning how to manage people the word way. Peter's emphasis, like a lot of other New Testament writers, is written more with the servant in mind, so we'll focus on the servant.

Here is a servant who might have a manager, who as far as he is concerned, is not cool by any stretch of the imagination. Let's even agree that this manager is a closer match to Al Capone and the Sicilian mafia godfather figure than anything else. This word-controlled servant is empowered by the word to remain good even if the manager is bad. It is interesting that so many word people will use the word to obtain healing and health but do not realise that the word can empower them to act appropriately in a sour relationship so they can influence people. The first instruction from Peter was not to quit our jobs because the manager is bad, but to release diligence as the word empowers us. We can be diligent even when treated badly. These managers are choosing to be bad because that is what they have in abundance in their heart. We are choosing to be diligent doers of the word because we are products of the word and are full of the word! It seems there is a scarcity of Christians who serve with a warrior's mentality.

The servant under discussion is suffering for doing right. Not all troubles are a result of our planting the wrong seeds in life. Are you facing a trouble? It does not mean you are wrong. The way the earth is organised, you can very well be doing what God says to do and contrary winds blow right in your face. This is not God's design, it is a result of the way man has organised the earth.

Just to be sure about what we are not discussing. A professional who goes for an all-night prayer meeting the day before a big presentation to a client is asking for trouble with management. It is really no business of his manager that this fellow chooses to leave from the office for a vigil, stay up all night and head back from the vigil to the office, but once he sets foot in that office he has signed up to a code of excellence. If his lack of sleep robs him of concentration and as a result he is unable to give a coherent presentation, his manager might breathe down his neck and the office becomes an extension of hell. Usually Christian professionals who will be gullible enough to act this way will also be prone to thinking that the devil is fighting them through their manager.

Such a believer has brought on himself the treatment that he is getting. He is suffering for doing wrong. The devil is not his problem; foolishness is waging war against him with spectacular success.

In context, the key thought presented in these verses is that we do not allow the way that people treat us change who we are or what we do. When we do what the word says, we are releasing the power of God into that situation.

Too many times Christians forget to act on the word when relationships go south. They resort to complaining and griping and then wonder why they feel so miserable and powerless.

Standing on the word in the midst of trouble

> [After all] what kind of glory [is there in it]
> if, when you do wrong and are punished
> for it, you take it patiently? But if you bear
> patiently with suffering [which results]
> when you do right and that is undeserved, it
> is acceptable and pleasing to God.
>
> 1 Peter 2:20 (Amplified)

Clearly there is a suffering that follows from doing wrong. That much is obvious. God by his Spirit is saying through Peter that it is perfectly possible to do the word of God and still suffer. In this verse, Peter is killing the sacred cow that we only have problems because we have personal sins.

Did Peter just combine the ideas of doing well and the experiencing of problems in the same sentence? It is possible to suffer specifically because you are doing what is right. Some people's theology does not really allow for this but we know, from the word, that one can suffer for doing right. Some dear Christians are perplexed that they are standing in faith and yet trouble came. Then, as is often the case, along comes some unwise person who failing to discern the situation assures them that if they really were a person of faith there will be no challenges. They conclude that the presence of challenges proves some faith deficiency.

Contrary to commonly held myths we do not suffer only because we do wrong. As you carry out your duties you are going to encounter things and sometimes people that impose themselves along your path. These are difficulties in the way.

> 16 Yet if any man suffer as a Christian, let him not be ashamed; but let him glorify God on this behalf.
> 19 Wherefore let them that suffer according to the will of God commit the keeping of their souls to him in well doing, as unto a faithful Creator.
> 1 Peter 4:16,19 (KJV)

If you are one of those people who equates suffering with being wrong, you will, like most people, be ashamed when an opportunity to suffer comes along. This type of suffering is the will of God. It means saying no to the flesh.

This suffering is not a reference to sickness or the likes, but it is a reference to choosing to stand on the word rather than giving the flesh first place.

It is as pleasing to God that we are delivered out of suffering as it is that there are sufferings that we go through by standing on the word doing what is right. The key thing is to know that you are acting on the word and are willing to stand forever on the truth of God. A man who is the righteousness of God in Christ is full of music even when things go tough. Those who interpret tough times to mean that they must have sinned will be scratching their heads looking for evidence that they are wrong once again. They are forever looking for evidence that they have blown it. People who are righteousness conscious are able to look past a tough situation and break forth into song because Jesus has released them from condemnation and shame.

How do I respond to an abusive master?

Or unto governors, as unto them that are
sent by him for the punishment of evildoers,
and for the praise of them that do well.
1 Peter 2:14 (KJV)

Trust good government and the authority structures that are in place. Stand on the word that authority structures will function according to God's word. Commend your soul to God who does right. When authority structures function right, the word is working and God is glorified. Whether or not the authority structures do right we stick to the word and choose to suffer wrong rather than retaliate with evil. Jesus and his encounter with the fig tree also illustrates how the existence of a problem does not mean that we are wrong.

> 20And in the morning, as they passed by, they saw the fig tree dried up from the roots.
> 21 And Peter calling to remembrance saith unto him, Master, behold, the fig tree which thou cursedst is withered away.
> 22 And Jesus answering saith unto them, Have faith in God.
> Mark 11:20-21 (KJV)

Peter said "Master look the fig tree is withered." Why did Peter not say this on the same day that Jesus cursed the fig tree? Peter had nothing to say because there was no observable change in the tree even after Jesus had spoken correctly to it. Peter was watching out for outcomes all the while and initially he saw none.

When Peter called Jesus' attention to the withered fig tree, it was because Peter's senses could finally see a withered tree. You see, when Jesus cursed that fig tree he had released the faith of God against that predicament. We know that Jesus had no faith impediment. He was obviously richly developed in faith. In that instance, faith was at work and yet there was a problem that lasted until the next morning. Anyone there would have thought that nothing had changed.

The truth is that faith was operating correctly and yet no one could see a difference. Jesus spoke to that tree in the morning, went about his daily tasks and it was not until the next morning that the tree was dried from the roots. Jesus has been practicing confession since he was a boy. He had almost 30 years of practice by the time he started speaking in public. Even then, the tree took 24 hours.

The point is that the tree had not instantly dematerialised. Jesus did not stand in the presence of that tree ashamed that he did not have instant results. He did not accept that as proof that he did not know what he was doing. He did not take the presence of that tree to mean that he must be deficient in faith. He simply allowed faith to continue to work while he went about his daily tasks. In time, others came to agree with him.

Consider Jairus the ruler of the synagogue, who approached Jesus concerning the healing of his daughter.

> 23 And besought him greatly, saying, My little daughter lieth at the point of death: I pray thee, come and lay thy hands on her, that she may be healed; and she shall live.
> 24 And Jesus went with him; and much people followed him, and thronged him.
> Mark 5:23-24 (KJV)

Jairus has approached Jesus with clearly stated expectations. He was correctly speaking his faith. He had placed a demand on God's power that was at work in the ministry of Jesus. You could say that he was cooperating with the power of God in the ministry of Jesus. Jairus believed that when hands were laid on his daughter she would be whole.

> While he yet spake, there came from the ruler of the synagogue's house certain which said, Thy daughter is dead: why troublest thou the Master any further?
> Mark 5:35 (KJV)

While Jesus and Jairus were headed out to Jairus house, news came that Jairus daughter was dead. So many people would have spent all their time wondering, worrying and investigating why the girl died. Faith does not spend its time doing this. We get ahead in life by knowing what we should do to reverse the situation rather than in investigating the origin of this challenge. If it were important to know the why, Jesus would have told Jairus. Jesus simply told Jairus to believe. The faith of Jairus was not deficient even though things had gone worse.

When the folks from Jairus' house counselled him not to trouble the master any further, they were saying to him that he should throw in the towel because his daughter is now dead. Jairus was still in faith. He had released his faith while the daughter was grievously sick, and now she is dead.

He had believed the word. He is walking with Jesus. The messenger comes along saying that things have changed for the worse!

His own people are saying in in a chorus "Jairus! Change!" The flesh and the world are united in their request "Jairus! change!" He was about to be blown away by anti-word sentiments!

He might be tempted to start investigating the cause of the daughter's death. If he did that, he would have compounded his paralysis because of too much analysis. He was simply to keep his faith switched on. He was not wrong. Nothing had changed except that things had gone worse in a turbulent world.

It is a strange fact, but the greatest challenge that we face when the going gets tough, is the problem of distraction. Too often we allow the presence of problems and well-meaning people lure us away from acting on what we already know in the word.

When the people said, "abandon ship, things have gone worse", Jesus' recommendation was to only believe. In other words Jairus you have done such a good job, you don't need to add anything or change your stance on the word. The word is working and the power of God is not short-circuited. Jesus in effect is telling him to stick with the word. "Hey Jairus there is a problem, but don't change your direction in the word because things have grown worse. Do not throw your hand up in shame thinking that you were deluded. We have seen the end of the story and we win! Just as you have stated, your daughter shall live."

We are not led by whether things have improved or gone worse. We follow the word. We listen to our spirits.

5 There shall not any man be able to stand before thee all the days of thy life: as I was with Moses, so I will be with thee: I will not fail thee, nor forsake thee.

6 Be strong and of a good courage: for unto this people shalt thou divide for an inheritance the land, which I sware unto their fathers to give them.

Joshua 1:5-6 (KJV)

When God tells Joshua "there shall not any man stand before you," God was forewarning Joshua that there would be challenges. The challenges were going to come about because Joshua is going to obey God and head towards the land of promise. He is in the very centre of God's will. There was nowhere else that God wanted Joshua to be, yet in the path of the pursuit of God's plan, there will be challenges. It is godly to know that trouble is coming before it arrives at your doorstep.

The advantage that Joshua has over many Christians today is that God warned him ahead of time. Today, God is not able to get that kind of message across to many people because the people that should give such warning are not preparing the people of God. Then on the other hand, folks are too condemnation-conscious. If they sense that problems are ahead, their belief system causes them to start condemning themselves that they must have missed it somewhere. The very message that God wanted to use to stir in them the warrior's mentality becomes what their flesh uses to destroy their confidence.

Godliness is not the absence of challenges. Challenges in themselves do not mean you are wrong. Too many times Christians are analysts, trying to find out why a challenge has come. We do not know why Jairus daughter died, nor do we know why the fig tree did not immediately dry up, but we know that Jairus faith and the power of God were undefeatable twin forces. We cannot always tell why people behave ugly, but we know to stand on the word and continue to do right. God's prescription still works, be strong and of good courage.

10

Conclusions

Supposing that the parable of the widow and the unjust judge is a directl representation of what God is like, there are some who teach that we should continuously approach God on a given matter in prayer until we weary him into acknowledging that we have a point. The thinking is that he responds to our cause when he sees our seriousness. They think that when God notices that we will not take a no for an answer, he responds by giving us a yes.

If Jesus taught us anything about prayer it is the truth that the Father does not respond to our repetition in prayer. We are sometimes encouraged to bombard the gates of heaven, but since God is our Father, which honorable son really bombards the gates of his father's house?

God does not want you to approach him as a widow in prayer. We approach him as our Father. We come boldly in the name of Jesus. We come as sons. Our identity in prayer is that of sons not widows!

The widow is coming to an unjust judge who sees her in cold detached terms. The widow is not related to the unjust judge. This is definitely unlike us for we are in the family of God. It is important to state once again that the parable illustrates how not to approach the Father God. We can expect much better treatment from God than the widow ever received from that cold, callous, godless, and loveless judge.

We do not approach our loving Father the way the woman approached the unjust judge. When you think of the unjust judge, just declare to yourself "this is not the picture of my heavenly Father who gave himself for me". The parable is a powerful contrast and not a description of God's modus operandi. God does not reason or operate like that unjust judge.

In the parable of the widow and the unjust judge, we are stoutly standing our grounds on the word of God and our understanding of his nature and unchanging attributes. The light that shines brightly from the revelation of God's goodness causes us to boldly affirm the truths that trigger the renewing of our minds.

As our mind becomes renewed, the reluctance and resistance breaks down and we have a window of opportunity to experience the answers that God's love has so lavishly released to us already in Christ.

Through this parable we see that the unrenewed mind is the number one reason for delays to the manifestation of God's word. WHat we do with our minds directly impacts how long the adversary, the thief is able to steal from us.

We also see that though there is an adversary who is clearly not for us but against us, he is not the main issue. At stake is whether you will relent in following through with your confession of the mighty truths of God's word who cannot lie.

> **The adversary seeks to cause you to believe that he rules outcomes. You are determined to reign and lord it over him through the word of God.**

The parable teaches arriving at a way of thinking and living by adopting a new way of speaking resting in the knowledge of a God who is pleased by your faith.

There are components of our constitution that are hard to be entreated and are slow to come into agreement with God's beautiful plan. We are not to give up when our soul brings up its tactics of delay. We know the word will trump at last! We can rest in the fact that entreating God is not a difficult task and never has been, no matter what religious spirits want us to believe about him. He is not waiting on us to persuade him and wear him out before he does us good. The God and Father of our Lord Jesus is far more willing than religion allows. Some think that God needs a lot of convincing before he showers us with his goodness. They buy into the idea that human pressure forces God to alter his course and change his mind. The thinking is that but for our insistent intervention through prayer, God was not going to show his good nature. It is that kind of philosophy that Jesus was dismantling with the aid of a well-crafted parable. Here is a thought that you must not forget and is the very point that Jesus is trying to get across.

> **If the unjust judge, who is not like God, will respond to the case of a widow who is unrelated to the judge then surely God will hear our prayers.**

You are related to God. He does not think of you as a widow. You are a joint heir, seated in the heavenlies with the Lord Jesus Christ.

Your job is to locate his will within his word and to keep that will in your heart by your saying it. God's word is the perfect image. It is the perfect seed. When you say it, you are keeping it in the heart. This changes your image. This seeing and saying is akin to watering the seed. If it remains planted in the heart and is allowed to seed the heart with new imagination it will ultimately release the results contained within the image as we renew our mind. The sentence that you are declaring already exists in the heart of God; you are not making anything up. You are not saying things just because they tickle your fancy.

> **When you confess God's word, you are causing what already exists in God in you to start to exist in your mind. The contagion of the word within your spirit infects the unjust judge of the mind until he comes into full agreement with you.**

When this gets to full maturity and the unjust judge is wearied, that which exists in God in you comes to exist in your experience. This is your victory experienced. God is infinitely satisfied in his own goodness, now it is your turn to maximize your satisfaction by resting in the goodness of God.

> But the Lord is faithful, who shall stablish
> you, and keep you from evil.
> 2 Thessalonians 3:3 (KJV)